Guidelines

VOL 24 / PART 1   January–April 2008

Edited by **Jeremy Duff and Katharine Dell**

Suggestions for using *Guidelines*

Set aside a regular time and place, if possible, when you can read and pray undisturbed. Before you begin, take time to be still and, if you find it helpful, use the BRF prayer.

In *Guidelines*, the introductory section provides context for the passages or themes to be studied, while the units of comment can be used daily, weekly, or whatever best fits your timetable. You will need a Bible (more than one if you want to compare different translations) as Bible passages are not included. At the end of each week is a 'Guidelines' section, offering further thoughts about, or practical application of what you have been studying.

You may find it helpful to keep a journal to record your thoughts about your study, or to note items for prayer. Another way of using *Guidelines* is to meet with others to discuss the material, either regularly or occasionally.

Occasionally, you may read something in *Guidelines* that you find particularly challenging, even uncomfortable. This is inevitable in a series of notes which draws on a wide spectrum of contributors, and doesn't believe in ducking difficult issues. Indeed, we believe that *Guidelines* readers much prefer thought-provoking material to a bland diet that only confirms what they already think.

If you do disagree with a contributor, you may find it helpful to go through these three steps. First, think about why you feel uncomfortable. Perhaps this is an idea that is new to you, or you are not happy at the way something has been expressed. Or there may be something more substantial—you may feel that the writer is guilty of sweeping generalization, factual error, theological or ethical misjudgment. Second, pray that God would use this disagreement to teach you more about his word and about yourself. Third, think about what you will do as a result of the disagreement. You might resolve to find out more about the issue, or write to the contributor or the editors of *Guidelines*. After all, we aim to be 'doers of the word', not just people who hold opinions about it.

Writers in this issue

Andrew Gregory is Chaplain of University College, Oxford. His publications include *Four Witnesses, One Gospel?* (Grove Books, 2005) and, as editor and contributor, *The Fourfold Gospel Commentary* (SPCK, 2006).

Paula Gooder teaches Biblical studies, both Old and New Testament, at the Queen's Ecumenical Theological Foundation, Birmingham, as well as working freelance as a biblical studies writer and lecturer. She is the author of *Hosea to Micah* in BRF's *People's Bible Commentary* series.

Janet Fletcher is a Team Vicar in the Walton Team, Honorary Chaplain of Liverpool Cathedral, and a spiritual director in Livrepool Diocese. She enjoys leading quiet days, retreats and study days on prayer and spirituality. Her book *Pathway to God: Following the Way in Prayer* was published in June 2006 (SPCK).

Alec Gilmore is a Baptist minister, writer and lecturer on biblical themes. He was formerly editor of Lutterworth Press and is the author of *A Dictionary of the English Bible and its Origins* (Continuum).

Christopher Hancock is the Director of the Centre for the Study of Christianity in China, Oxford. He was previously Dean of Bradford Cathedral, Vicar of Holy Trinity Church, Cambridge, and for ten years an academic theologian teaching at Virginia Theological Seminary and the University of Cambridge. In his new work, Chris travels and teaches extensively in China and Asia.

Jenny Hellyer is a spiritual director, musician, clergy wife and mother based in Oxford. After teaching and theological study, she was part of the Lee Abbey Community in Devon for seven years.

Henry Wansbrough OSB, after 14 years on the Theology Faculty of Oxford University, has returned to his monastery in Yorkshire, where he is leading a course for MA in Theology.

Mark Powley is an Associate Pastor at St Paul's, Hammersmith. He is the author of the discipleship guide *4Life* (Cell UK, 2006) and helped to found *Breathe*, a network for Christian living in consumer culture (visit www.ibreathe.org.uk).

Further BRF reading for this issue

For more in-depth coverage of some of the passages in these
Bible reading notes, we recommend the following titles:

978 1 84101 092 2, £7.99

978 1 84101 242 1, £8.99

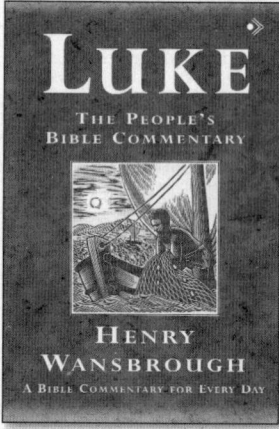

978 1 84101 027 8, £7.99

978 1 84101 094 6, £7.99

The Editors write...

New life through suffering is an important biblical theme. Often we shy away from it, preferring just the victory, but repeatedly the message is that progress, whether in understanding, release from oppression or closeness to God, comes through hardship. It's a theme that runs through this issue of *Guidelines*.

We begin with Jesus' road to the cross, the third instalment of Andrew Gregory's notes on Luke's Gospel. The end point is the resurrection, but the journey to it is through suffering. Then with Paula Gooder we look at the character of Esther, a great heroine of the Jewish people at a time of severe threat. A new writer, Janet Fletcher, then leads us in two weeks looking at prayer—how we can respond to God's call to pray for ourselves and the world around us in all its difficulties, and to meet with him.

Next, we turn to the theme of wilderness, which Alec Gilmore tackles mainly from an Old Testament perspective but including important passages from the New involving Jesus and John the Baptist. Wilderness has been described as 'the single most informative experience in the creation of the Jewish people' (Carol Ochs) and is as profound a source of spiritual inspiration today as it was to the people of Israel. We spend Holy Week in the company of Christopher Hancock, as we see

Jesus on the road to the crucifixion and through that terrible suffering. The following week, guided by Jenny Hellyer, we see how Jesus' resurrection towers over history, yet also transforms individual lives.

Finally we come to Job and 1 and 2 Peter. Henry Wansbrough covers the ever-fascinating book of Job, which goes to the heart of the very human issues of innocent suffering, just retribution and relationship with God. Why do people suffer? Are there any rewards for good behaviour? If unjust suffering is from God, how do we understand our relationship with him? Mark Powley's notes on 1 and 2 Peter challenge us with the vision of Christians living in exile in a world estranged from God: how to live, how to live well, and how to survive when all is against you. This issue starts with Jesus' example—suffering followed by vindication—and it concludes with this call from Peter to model our lives on the same pattern.

Katharine Dell, Jeremy Duff

5

The BRF Prayer

Almighty God,
you have taught us that your word is a lamp for our
feet and a light for our path. Help us, and all who
prayerfully read your word, to deepen our
fellowship with each other through your love. And
in so doing may we come to know you more fully,
love you more truly, and follow more faithfully in
the steps of your son Jesus Christ, who lives and
reigns with you and the Holy Spirit,
one God for evermore. Amen.

LUKE 19:28—24:53

This is the third and final part of our encounter with the Gospel according to Luke. In the first part of our reading of Luke's orderly account (1:3), we read the opening chapters of his narrative (1:1—9:50). They told us parts of the story of Jesus prior to his public ministry and offered us glimpses of his ministry in Galilee. In the second part, we followed Jesus and his disciples on their journey from Galilee to Jerusalem (9:51—19:27). Now we arrive with them in that city, the place where prophets must die and to which Jesus has come in order that he may be taken up (9:51). Here he will undergo great suffering, be rejected by the Jewish religious leaders, be killed, and on the third day be raised (9:22; cf. 24:46). Here he will accomplish his departure (9:31; cf. 24:51), and from here his disciples will, in Jesus' name, proclaim repentance and forgiveness of sins to all nations (24:47; cf. 2:30–32).

Closely related to Luke's emphasis on Jerusalem is his interest in the temple. Luke's first volume both begins and ends there (1:5–23; 24:53). Twice already he has told us about Jesus being brought to the temple as a child (2:22–37, 41–50). Now Jesus goes to the temple again, and those who hear him teach are spellbound by what he says (19:47–48). Luke emphasizes Jesus' teaching in the temple, and it provides the setting for everything that takes place in Jerusalem before Jesus' arrest (19:45—20:1; 21:1–5, 37–38).

Luke's account moves next to the events that lead from Jesus' suffering and death (chs. 22—23) to his consequent exaltation (ch. 24). Here, as also in Luke's presentation of Jesus and his teaching in the temple, a number of distinctive Lukan themes and interests are present.

In chapters 22 and 23, Luke shows more variation from Mark, in order and content, than he does in other parts of his Gospel where he and Mark write about the same events. Luke omits from his passion narrative many elements that are present in Mark, and also includes quite a lot of material that is not found in Mark. This has led some scholars to ask whether Luke might have had another continuous written passion source besides the account given by Mark. Another possibility is that, in this part of his Gospel, Luke has used Mark more freely than he did elsewhere, which may be explained by the particular concerns that drove him to narrate his own orderly account. Either way, those passages that are found only in Luke may play an important role in determining why Luke wrote his passion narrative in the way that he did. This in turn may help us to see how Luke thought that his passion narrative would help us to live as followers of the crucified, risen and ascended Jesus Christ.

---

1 Approaching the city

Luke 19:28–40

Luke takes care to ensure that his readers will grasp the significance of Jesus' entry into Jerusalem. By making an explicit link between Jesus' journey to Jerusalem and the parable he has just told (v. 28), Luke invites us to understand Jesus' journey in the light of this story about someone having been made king, who returns to his subjects and calls them to account (19:11–27). Clearer still is Luke's explicit reference to Jesus as king, placed on the lips of the crowd (v. 38).

Jesus' kingship is of a very particular type. At no point in Jerusalem will he assert his royal status, although the crowds who acclaim him as king are correct to do so. They recognize the truth of what Mary and we, the readers of Luke's Gospel, were told long ago (1:32). The way that Jesus rides on a colt is surely symbolic. Matthew and John refer explicitly to Zechariah 9:9, but Luke makes the same point implicitly: Jesus is a king who is not only triumphant and victorious but also humble.

Luke's introduction of the Pharisees who call upon Jesus to rebuke the crowds is striking. It introduces a discordant note. Not all who see Jesus grasp who he is; not all acclaim him as king. Luke has always made clear that there will be different responses to Jesus, from the moment that his parents first brought him to the temple (2:34). Now, as Jesus approaches the temple once more, the opposition of some Pharisees reminds us that different people respond to Jesus in different ways. There will always be those who resist God's rule or fail to recognize it when they see it (19:44), but no amount of opposition can suppress the truth of who Jesus is (v. 40).

2 Challenging the temple

Jesus comes to Jerusalem not only as a king but also as a prophet. Others may rejoice at his coming but Jesus weeps as he reflects on what will happen to the city. He weeps not for himself but for Jerusalem. We are reminded of his earlier lament over the city (13:34–35), but now Jesus' words are presented with greater emotional intensity. Jesus does not shrink from speaking of judgment, but takes no pleasure from the prospect of what will befall the city in which he himself will be killed. Nor does Luke, who almost certainly wrote his Gospel after Jerusalem had been destroyed in AD70.

Luke moves from his account of Jesus' lament when Jesus was still outside the city to Jesus' entry into the temple. This accentuates the point that the city and the temple are as one, and may be intended to show how Jesus fulfils the words of the prophet Malachi: 'the Lord whom you seek will suddenly come to his temple' (3:1–5). Jesus acts with the same prophetic authority that he showed when he wept for the city. In the Old Testament, prophets frequently denounced what they saw as the corruption of the temple; Jesus follows their example, quoting Isaiah and Jeremiah as he does so.

The two elements on which Luke focuses are typical of his presentation of Jesus. One is the importance of prayer (v. 46a, probably alluding to Isaiah 56:7). The other is the proper use of money and material things (v. 46b, drawn from Jeremiah 7:11, part of a passage in which Jeremiah rails against worshippers who desecrate the temple). Luke's account of Jesus' action is less detailed and less violent than those of the other Gospel writers. He focuses on what Jesus says rather than what he does, and presents Jesus as continuing to teach daily in the temple (v. 47), even after he has spoken out against the way in which it was being used.

Those who hear Jesus continue to respond in different ways: the people hang upon Jesus' words, but their leaders seek a way to kill him.

We are unlikely to identify ourselves with the latter—but does our commitment to prayer and the proper use of our material goods demonstrate that we hear and act on what Jesus teaches?

3 The teacher in the temple

Luke 20:1–8

Luke puts great emphasis on Jesus' teaching in the temple, over what appears to be a significant period (19:47; 21:37–38; 22:53). It is in response to this teaching that the religious leaders challenge Jesus about what he is doing and the authority on which his teaching rests. (In Luke's account, 'these things', v. 2, refers most naturally to what Jesus was saying on the occasion that he was challenged by the chief priests, scribes and elders—not to the cleansing of the temple, which took place on an earlier occasion.) This encounter paves the way for continuing controversy between Jesus and those associated with the temple.

Jesus both avoids and answers the question that is put to him. When he is first challenged about the authority on which his teaching rests, he counters by asking his questioners how they judged John the Baptist, another preacher with widespread popular support. Their refusal to answer Jesus' question means that Jesus will not answer their question either, but his reference to John strongly implies that Jesus' authority depends on the same source as had John's. Each is a prophet sent by God. But those who remember John's teaching will recall that he spoke of someone coming who was more powerful than he (3:16–17). That 'more powerful' one has now arrived, but those responsible for the temple to which he has come do not recognize who he is. They do not recognize the time of their visitation from God (19:44).

4 Turning on the tenants

Luke 20:9–19

Jesus may speak this parable to the people (v. 9), but his real targets are the Jerusalem authorities, as they are well aware (v. 19). Thus Jesus continues the debate that he has been having with them about the authority on which he teaches and preaches.

The parable clearly functions as an allegory of the sending of Jesus to the people of Israel. The vineyard stands for Israel (see Isaiah 5:1–7) and the beloved son for Jesus (Luke 3:22). As Luke presents it, the parable is like a self-fulfilling prophecy. Jesus indicates what will happen to him (v. 15), and those to whom he directs the parable are given further reason to try to kill him (v. 19). Their actions will contribute to the transfer of the vineyard from one set of owners to another. Thus this parable both encapsulates and contributes to the events that Luke narrates.

The parable of the vineyard is found also in the Gospels according to Matthew and Mark, as well as in the Gospel of Thomas. What is most distinctive about Luke's version is the way in which he draws further attention to the stone that the builders rejected (v. 17), by expanding on its significance in verse 18. Here Jesus speaks of two additional functions of the cornerstone besides its normal use, which was to bear the weight or stress of two walls and so hold a structure together. Such a stone would not be expected to move; nor was it usually in a position where people could trip over it. Luke suggests not only that it may cause others to stumble (probably an allusion to Isaiah 8:14–15) but also that it may fall upon them. In either case, this stone destroys those who come into conflict with it.

Luke emphasizes the serious consequences that rejecting Jesus entails, but he also makes clear that it is the Jewish leaders of the time, not the Jewish people as a whole, who will be judged for rejecting Jesus (v. 19). So too we must remember the grief with which Jesus contemplated the fate of Jerusalem (19:41–44). Luke leaves no room for Christian triumphalism.

5 Two trick questions

Luke 20:20–40

Jesus' opponents try to trap him with trick questions. The chief priests ask about politics and the Sadducees about theology, but Jesus foils them both.

It is hard to know whether or not Jesus' words about giving to Caesar and to God what belongs to each are really intended to address questions about how Jesus' followers should relate to the demands of the state alongside the demands of God. It is perhaps more likely that they are a clever response allowing Jesus to escape the trap that has been set for him, and to show that his opponents already use coins on which Caesar's image is stamped. Certainly it seems unlikely that Jesus would equate Caesar and God as two parallel kings, each equally deserving of our obedience. We who are stamped with the image of God owe our allegiance to him. It is significant, however, that Jesus does not forbid the paying of taxes to Caesar (v. 25), something of which he will later be accused (23:2).

Jesus' answer to the second question put to him (by the Sadducees) is as unexpected as was his answer to the first. This time, however, it is clearly the outworking of a definite theological conviction about what belief in the resurrection of the dead entails. Only very rarely is there any clear reference to belief in the resurrection in the Old Testament, so most scholars agree that this belief developed only after most of the Old Testament had been written. Many Jews from before and during the time of Jesus did believe in the resurrection of the dead, but the conservative Sadducees did not. Thus their question about whose wife this woman would be after she and her late husbands were raised is designed to demonstrate that the very belief in resurrection is ridiculous. Jesus' answer denies that this is the case. He suggests that the problem identified by the Sadducees exists only because they do not grasp what a huge transformation the resurrection will bring. Old relationships will be no more, for God will do something new.

These Sadducees were mistaken in believing that the life of those raised from the dead will be little different from the life that we experience today. Jesus challenges them and us to see that the resurrection will bring life of an altogether new kind, a life in which we will be like angels, true children of God. We shall not merely be resurrected corpses, still encumbered by obligations incurred in this mortal life.

6 Scribes and widows

Luke 20:41—21:4

Jesus continues his teaching, but now it is he who takes the initiative. Psalm 110, which Jesus quotes here, is one of a group of texts known as the royal psalms. It was probably written to be used at the coronation of a king in the Davidic dynasty. Jesus ascribes the psalm to David, its traditional author, and so uses the psalm to pose a question. 'Lord' is the title that sons should give to their father, not vice versa. How, then, can David speak of his son, or descendant, as his lord? Elsewhere Luke makes clear that Jesus is descended from David (1:32–33; 3:31). Here Jesus does not call that understanding into question, but does imply that he is not merely a human son of David; he is more important than David, which is why the psalm refers to him as David's lord. Perhaps Jesus is suggesting that 'lord' is a better title to use, or a better way to think of him, than 'son of David' (see Acts 2:36).

Jesus turns from questioning his opponents about the way in which they interpret scripture (vv. 41–44) to criticizing them for the way in which they lead their lives (vv. 45–47). They seek honour and respect in public, yet are part of a system that preys on vulnerable and needy figures, such as widows. Exactly how they 'devoured' widows is not made clear, but the contrast between widows as the victims of oppression (20:47) and a widow who symbolizes those who give to God, rather than expecting to receive from him (21:2), is striking.

One way that we might read this widow's story is to say that she gives generously and sacrificially, and that Jesus uses her example to challenge us to do the same. But Jesus does not praise her or refer to her as an example to follow, so to assume that this is what he meant may be to miss the point. Jesus has just condemned religious leaders for seeking respect while devouring widows' houses. Is this particular widow another of their victims? Is she a victim of a religious system that takes money from the poor to give to the rich rather than vice versa, a system that claims divine authorization for such reprehensible behaviour? Earlier, Jesus challenged those who had made the temple a den of robbers (19:46). Here he seems to be making a similar point. Unscrupulous religious leaders had taken something good—the temple treasury—and turned it into something bad, something that took from the very people whom it was intended to support. Is this a risk that we might run in our churches, our families or elsewhere?

Guidelines

Although Christians have played a full and sometimes shameful part in struggles over Jerusalem, it is striking how little attention they have paid to the site on which Herod's temple once stood and the Dome of the Rock stands today. Known to Jews as the Temple Mount and to Muslims as the Haram esh-Sharif, claims about this site, or actions on, under or around it, may have repercussions that are felt all around the world.

Christian interest in Jerusalem has largely been focused elsewhere. The very fact that Muslims built the Dome of the Rock on this site reminds us that Christians built nothing there in the centuries when they controlled Jerusalem. In one way, this is something that should disturb us. Christians from the fourth century left the temple ruins alone because they wanted to be reminded of its destruction as a sign of God's judgment on his people for rejecting Jesus. Such beliefs now seem vindictive, and no doubt played a part in the terrible anti-Semitism to which the Church has sometimes contributed. Yet there are other reasons why Christians have not focused their interest on the Temple Mount. Positively put, the lack of Christian interest in this site is but the consequence of the belief that God's presence on earth reached its definitive focus not in a place but in a person.

Time and time again in the Hebrew Bible, God's prophets attacked the way in which the temple was run, claiming that the sacrificial system at the heart of Jewish identity had lost sight of why it was there in the first place. Jesus does something similar when he takes his place in a long line of prophetic protest against the temple system. Jesus the Jew enters an intra-Jewish debate when he cleanses the temple, but Luke and the other Gospel writers make clear that something new is also at stake. God's presence is no longer focused in the temple, but in Jesus and in the Spirit whom he will send.

1 Destruction foretold

Luke 21:5–24

Comments about the beauty of the temple, as it then was, lead Jesus to move from condemning the way in which it was run to warning of the destruction that awaits it (vv. 5–6). He speaks both of cataclysmic events that will shake the world (vv. 9–11) and of persecution that will come upon the Church (vv. 12–19). These events are terrible, but they do not mean that the end of the world is nigh (v. 9). The fate of Jerusalem does not suggest any such thing, either, for it may be in non-Jewish hands for some time (vv. 20–24). Jesus speaks of earthly events that are yet to take place, but Luke almost certainly wrote his Gospel after Jerusalem had been destroyed by the Romans. Thus, Luke knows that followers of Jesus had already found themselves handed over to Jewish and Roman authorities and brought before kings and governors—as had Jesus himself. The story of how this will happen to Jesus follows now in Luke. The story of how it happened also to his disciples is told in Acts.

The double perspective that we find here—Jesus speaking of the future but Luke writing about the past—helps to draw us into Luke's story. Jesus' authority is underlined, for we see how the events he prophesied have been fulfilled; and we are encouraged, for we too may take our stand for Christ alongside those who have done so already. Luke has Jesus speak of those who will be hated because of his name (v. 17). This is a fate that many readers of these notes will be spared, but countless other Christians have not been so lucky. Remembering their plight should drive us not only to pray for the many Christians who suffer for Jesus' name today, but also to work in support of freedom of expression for Christians, as well as for those of other religions or ideological commitments who are persecuted on account of their beliefs.

2 Glory and vindication

Jesus' reference to signs in the heavens (v. 25) brings us back to the question that was put to him in 21:7. But it is far from clear whether Jesus is moving on to speak of the final judgment, or whether he is still talking about the complex of events that will include Jerusalem's rejection of Jesus and its resulting destruction. Certainly Luke believed that the risen Jesus would one day return (Acts 1:11), but whether he is referring here to that belief is by no means certain.

One way to read Jesus' reference to the Son of Man coming in a cloud with power and great glory (v. 27, quoting Daniel 7:13) is to interpret it as a reference to the second coming. That is how it has often been understood, but there are problems with reading the verse in this way. Jesus says that all this will take place before 'this generation' has passed away (v. 32). Jesus' audience (and Luke's original readers) are long since dead, but Jesus has not returned. Does this mean that Jesus was mistaken? Or might it mean that he was talking about something that has already happened as he said that it would? It is possible—and perhaps better—to read this passage in this way. Jesus quotes from Daniel 7, a scene that describes a battle being fought in heaven. There in heaven, the 'Ancient of Days', the God of the universe, is seated on his throne. Then, on the clouds of heaven, comes 'one like a son of man'. He approaches the Ancient of Days and is led into his presence. There he is given authority, glory and sovereign power, and is worshipped by people of every language. This, says Jesus, is what will happen to him, just as surely as Jerusalem will be destroyed. Thus he is referring to his vindication before God after his death and ascension, not to his coming again to earth as judge.

We, the readers of Luke, may be confident that just as surely as Jerusalem was destroyed, so Jesus is enthroned on high. Just as surely as Jerusalem has fallen, so the crucified and risen Jesus has come before the throne of God, and has been exalted there as our king. No matter what terrible things happen, even in them and through them God will work his purpose out. Hold on to this, and we will have strength to maintain faith in an often hostile and inhospitable world. Hold on to this, and we will see how things truly are. What happens in heaven determines what will happen here on earth. Jesus has ascended to his Father's throne, and from there he has given us God's Spirit through whom he is present with us today (Luke 24:49; Acts 2:33).

3 Preparing for the Passover

Luke 22:1–13

Luke turns now from his account of Jesus' teaching in the temple to the beginning of his account of Jesus' passion. Thus Luke introduces here the three intertwining factors that will lead to Jesus' death on a Roman cross. Two are obvious—the enmity of the chief priests and scribes (clearly distinguished from the Jewish people as a whole, v. 2), who are looking for a way to put Jesus to death, and the action of Judas, one of the Twelve but now possessed by Satan (v. 3). He will hand Jesus over to the Jewish authorities, who will in turn hand Jesus over to the Romans. Had Satan not entered Judas, Luke perhaps implies, Jesus may not have been crucified.

Yet a third factor must also be considered, which is not made explicit in the verses that we read today, but lies at the heart of the narrative that Luke presents. Although the Satan-possessed Judas may conspire with Jesus' human opponents to find a way to put him to death, the end that they will achieve is no less than the will of God. Jesus has been travelling purposefully to Jerusalem in order that there he may be taken up (9:51). Now the climax of his journey is at hand. The events that will befall him are no accident but the will of God. Just as the Passover lamb had to be sacrificed (v. 8), so too must Jesus be sacrificed for others. Luke will make this clear in his account of the last supper; now he shows how Jesus continues to take the initiative (vv. 8–12), even as others conspire against him. Previously, Jesus had sent two disciples ahead to find the colt on which he would enter Jerusalem; now he sends his two closest disciples to prepare for the Passover meal at which he will speak more of his fate. Luke's comment that the disciples find everything just as Jesus had told them (v. 13) is the first of several occasions in the passion narrative when he emphasizes that Jesus is in control of what is unfolding, despite any appearance to the contrary. Even when the worst seems to happen, even when Satan seems to be winning, God remains in control.

4 Poured out for us

Luke 22:14–23

Luke presents his fullest explanation of the meaning of Jesus' death in his account of the last supper, which he clearly presents in the context of a Passover meal. Passover is the annual festival that celebrates and retells the story of God's deliverance of Israel from Egypt, made possible because the angel of death 'passed over' the firstborn of Israel who were protected by the blood of a lamb (see Exodus 12:1–28). The belief that Jesus was the Passover lamb goes back to our earliest Christian author, Paul, whose own account of the last supper shares important parallels with the account found in Luke (see 1 Corinthians 5:7; 11:23–27).

Jesus' words to those gathered with him speak of both his body and his blood, symbolized by the bread and wine that he gives to his disciples. His body is 'given for you'; his blood is 'poured out for you' as 'the new covenant' (vv. 19–20). Luke alone presents Jesus as referring to his body as 'given for you', although Paul says something very similar in 1 Corinthians 11:24. By presenting Jesus in this way, Luke suggests the sacrificial nature of Jesus' self-offering. The same is true of the language of a cup being 'poured out', for wine was often poured out as a sacrifice. Jesus' reference to a new covenant may echo God's promise that he would act to make a new covenant, written on his people's hearts (Jeremiah 31:31–34), but the fact that this new covenant is 'in his blood' makes it more likely that the allusion is to Exodus 24:8. Either way, Jesus' death will achieve something new, something that is offered to us—the possibility of a new, restored relationship with God, who has taken the initiative to draw us closer to him.

Once again, Luke makes it clear that Jesus' death is not an accident but the plan of God. Jesus takes his place at the table 'when the hour came' (v. 14; cf. Luke 22:53; John 13:1) and will go 'as it has been determined' (v. 22). Also important is the way in which Judas' action is described. He is sometimes said to 'betray' Jesus, but the verb may just as easily—and probably better—be translated as 'hand over' (v. 22; see also vv. 4, 6). This is the same verb that Paul uses to refer to God 'handing over' Jesus for our salvation (for example, Romans 8:32; 4:25), so Luke's use of the word may reflect the very early conviction that just as Jesus willingly gave himself for us, so God willingly gave his Son. This gives us reason not only to remember (v. 19) but also to rejoice—to eat and drink in remembrance that Christ died for us, and to be thankful.

5 Among us as one who serves

Luke 22:24–38

Only one disciple will hand over Jesus to his enemies, but here we see that none of them has yet grasped the nature of the role to which Jesus has called them. Their reaction to the news that one of them will betray them is to compete among themselves over who is Jesus' greatest disciple (v. 24), as opposed to the 'worst' one whose identity remains unknown (22:23).

Jesus' response to their dispute over status is to offer two contrasting models of how authority may be exercised. One way, that of earthly rulers who flaunt their power and seek recognition from others (v. 25), is as recognizable today as it was to Jesus' contemporaries. This way is to be rejected. The other way, the way in which the greater lives as if he were the lesser, and the one who leads becomes the one who serves, is modelled by Jesus himself. The point that John portrays by means of a story (John 13:3–16), Luke portrays in one telling and memorable phrase. Jesus is among his disciples 'as one who serves' (v. 27; cf. 12:37), and all who seek to exercise authority in his name should exercise it as he did— through service to others. That is how it will be in God's kingdom, and that is how those who remain with Jesus must continue to act.

Jesus speaks of himself not only as the one who serves but also as the one in whom scripture finds its fulfilment (v. 37). The passage that he quotes is Isaiah 53:12, which will shortly be fulfilled when Jesus is arrested as a bandit (22:53) and crucified between two criminals (23:32). Perhaps there is a deeper meaning as well: throughout his ministry Jesus has associated with those whom others counted as lawless or sinners, so the hostility that he faces now is little different from the hostility that he has encountered before (7:34; 15:1–2; 19:7–10). Once again Luke reminds us that Jesus' death is the outworking of the eternal purpose of God. His death is no mistake but the inevitable consequence of the life that Jesus led among us as one who serves.

6 The struggle to obey

Luke 22:39–46

Luke's account of Jesus' prayer and anguish in Gethsemane focuses on Jesus' relationship to his Father and the costly obedience it entails, not on Jesus' reaction when he finds his disciples asleep. They are to pray that they will not themselves come into the time of trial (vv. 40, 46; cf. 11:4), although Jesus knows that his own trial is about to begin (v. 42; cf. 9:22; 18:31–33). The way in which Jesus thinks of the needs of others rather than focusing on his own is reminiscent of the way in which he will later pray for forgiveness for those who crucify him (23:34).

Verses 43–44 are among a number of places towards the end of Luke where there are significant variations between early manuscripts that contain this Gospel. Some manuscripts contain these verses but others do not. This is why some English translations relegate them to a footnote (for example, RSV), or print them in square brackets (for example, NRSV). The evidence of different manuscripts is finely balanced, and specialists continue to disagree, but various reasons support an increasing tendency among scholars to consider these verses an authentic part of the Gospel. Central to the debate is a proper understanding of the word in verse 44 that has been translated 'agony' (RSV) and 'anguish' (NRSV, NIV) but might also be translated 'struggle' or 'trial'. Jesus experiences a mixture of doubt and faith as he prays, but moves to an acceptance of his Father's will (v. 42). It is in response to his prayer that an angel comes to strengthen him for the struggle that still lies ahead (vv. 43–44), just as it was in response to Jesus' prayer that God sent his Spirit to empower him for his forthcoming ministry (3:21–22). God answers Jesus' prayer by giving him strength for his ordeal, not by removing the cup that he must drink.

Luke's portrayal of Jesus in the garden points clearly to the cost of what he is about to undergo. Jesus shares our natural and very human tendency to wish to avoid suffering and death, but as he prays he is enabled to accept the will of God. On one level, Luke offers us Jesus as an example to follow. Most of all, however, he emphasizes Jesus' obedience to his Father's will. Thus Luke prepares us to watch with gratitude and awe as Jesus enters into his time of trial.

Guidelines

In the garden of Gethsemane, as in the wilderness (4:1–13), Jesus enters into a time of testing. In each instance, Luke's focus is on the person of Jesus. Each scene is concerned primarily to show us the sort of obedient son that Jesus is, not to present us with a model of how to respond when we find ourselves tried or tested. Jesus is willingly tested but tells the disciples in the garden to pray that they may escape the time of trial (22:40), just as he includes this petition in the prayer he gives to all his disciples (11:4). It is through Jesus' testing and obedience, not ours, that we are offered salvation.

The writer to the Hebrews puts it like this: 'In the days of his flesh, Jesus offered up prayers and supplications, with loud cries and tears, to the one who was able to save him from death, and he was heard because of his reverent submission. Although he was a Son, he learned obedience through what he suffered; and having been made perfect, he became the source of eternal salvation for all who obey him' (5:7–9).

1 A kiss in the darkness

Luke 22:47–53

Jesus' acceptance of God's will for his life and of the fate to which it will lead allows him to remain in control when Judas and the accompanying crowds come to arrest him. Jesus' disciples are thrown into confusion and resort to violence, but Jesus takes and retains the initiative. He speaks to Judas, forbids his disciples from further resistance and heals the slave whom they have wounded. Even now, at the moment of his arrest, Jesus shows compassion for others. His mercy and healing are extended even to his enemies, even when his own time of trial has begun.

The identification of those who accompany Judas and the crowds as the 'chief priests, the officers of the temple police, and the elders' (v. 52) reminds us that those most strongly opposed to Jesus were those whose authority and status were vested in the temple. Previously, in daylight, the favour that Jesus had found with the crowds meant that these authorities could not move against him. Now, at night, the crowds accompany Jesus' opponents as they come to arrest him.

Jesus' words to the religious leaders are both ironic and chilling. Who are the bandits/robbers (v. 52; cf. 19:46)? It is the religious leaders who have come armed with swords and clubs, while Jesus counteracts the violence done by his apostles (vv. 51–52). The fact that the power of darkness (v. 53) has come upon the temple and its rulers is a warning to all who claim to serve and worship God. Might we, too, fail to recognize God even when he is closest? Might we, too, be so overcome by darkness, even where God's presence should be clearest, that we fail to recognize, receive and rejoice in the light that he sends?

2 The prophet mocked

Luke 22:54–71

Peter's denial of Jesus reminds us that Judas was not the only disciple who failed to follow the master to the goal of his journey. Just as Peter failed to pray that he would not enter into the time of trial (22:46), so he fails when the moment of trial comes. But Luke implies that this is not the end of the story for Peter. Just as Jesus taught his disciples to forgive without counting, so Jesus forgives Peter even when he denies him three times. Peter's cowardice in the courtyard fulfils the prophetic 'word of the Lord' (v. 61) that Jesus had spoken (v. 61; 22:31–34), so we may be sure that Peter will yet turn back and serve Jesus faithfully once again. Though his tears are bitter (v. 62), they may indicate Peter's repentance and point to what he will go on to do.

Peter recognizes Jesus as a prophet, but those who mock, beat and ridicule him and those who try him (vv. 63–71) do not. Jesus appears to remain silent when he is mocked. Before the Council, he gives only partial and indirect answers to the questions that he is asked. Jesus neither affirms nor denies that he is Messiah and Son of God, although this is what the angel declared of him even before he was born (1:32, 35). What Jesus does affirm, however, is his rightful place sitting at the right hand of God (v. 69). This is an allusion to Psalm 110:1, which is used here (as frequently in the New Testament) to refer to Jesus' resurrection and his exaltation into heaven. Even when on trial for his life, Jesus remains confident that he has come to Jerusalem in order to be taken up (9:51).

There is a great deal of irony in the exchange between Jesus and his accusers. It is they who ask if Jesus is Messiah and say that he is the Son of God, even if they do not believe it. Jesus does not claim that they are right, for that would be to fall into their trap and give his accusers a clear charge to bring against him. Thus Jesus remains in control of the situation, even when under arrest. But we who read the Gospel know that Jesus' accusers are correct in what they say. In this scene, Luke suggests that the real reason that Jesus is on trial is the question of his relationship to God. Only when he is brought before Pilate will political accusations be made.

3 Innocent on all counts

Luke 23:1–12

Jesus' trial before Pilate is as brief as was his trial before the Sanhedrin, but the charges now brought against him (v. 2) are new, political, and clearly false. Jesus neither forbade people to pay tax to the emperor (20:20–25) nor declared that he was the Messiah, a king (22:67–69). Luke contrasts the duplicity and insistence (vv. 2, 5) of the Jewish leaders that Jesus be found guilty with the indifference of Pilate, who finds no basis for the accusation against him (v. 4). Luke's point that even Pilate could find no crime with which to charge Jesus is in keeping with other encounters with Roman officials that he depicts in Acts. Just as, here, he suggests that Jesus was no threat to Rome, so there he makes a similar point about Jesus' followers.

The charge that Jesus stirred up trouble in Galilee allows Pilate to send Jesus to Herod. Luke is the only author of a New Testament Gospel who includes this episode. Luke shows a lot of interest in Herod, and clearly he thought that this incident was important, for he returns to it in one of Peter's speeches in Acts (4:27). There Peter claimed that Pilate's collaboration with Herod was in fulfilment of Psalm 2:1–2, which speaks of kings and rulers conspiring against the Lord and his Messiah. This is a good example of the way in which Luke's knowledge of Jewish scripture shapes the way in which he presents his orderly account of the story of Jesus.

The inclusion of Herod serves also to accentuate Luke's negative portrayal of the Jewish leaders who plot against Jesus. Luke knows that Herod was as brutal a ruler as was Pilate (9:9; 13:1–2), yet Herod also finds no charge to bring against Jesus (23:15). Thus, two authorities testify to Jesus' innocence, contrary to the charges brought against him. Luke's statement that Herod and Pilate thus became friends rather than enemies (v. 12) is intriguing. Could this be an example of the presence of Jesus leading to reconciliation, albeit between brutal rulers whom Luke portrays as lacking the courage of their convictions?

4 He suffered under Pontius Pilate...

Luke 23:13–31

Luke continues to develop the intertwined themes of Jesus' innocence (vv. 14–15, 22) and the contrast with the Jewish leaders (now joined by the people: vv. 13, 18). It is Pilate's verdict that sends Jesus to his death but Luke makes clear his conviction that the religious authorities were the driving force behind Jesus' crucifixion. Pilate hands Jesus over (v. 25), as previously did Judas. So too, of course, did God (see notes on 22:14–23).

Yet not all the Jewish people follow their leaders in wishing to see Jesus killed. A great number of the people follow Jesus, among them women who weep for his misfortune (v. 27). Although on the way to his own death, Jesus has compassion for them. They are innocent of his death, as are their children, yet they will be caught up in the calamity to which his death will lead (vv. 28–31; cf. 19:41–44; 21:20–44). Just as the women mourn in advance of Jesus' impending death, so Jesus mourns in advance of Jerusalem's impending destruction. He takes no pleasure in disaster befalling others.

Jesus has journeyed to Jerusalem and was greeted on his arrival as the king who came in the name of the Lord (19:38). Now he journeys on the way of the cross and will be mocked as the king of the Jews (23:36, 38). We are not told whether Simon of Cyrene willingly carried Jesus' cross, but Luke's description of him carrying it 'behind/after Jesus' (v. 26) may be suggestive. Simon's action reminds us of what Jesus demands of those who want to become his disciples: that we deny ourselves, take up our cross daily and follow him (9:23). If we fail to do so, we cannot be his disciples (14:27).

5 ... was crucified...

Luke 23:32–43

Just as the Jewish people are divided in their response to Jesus, so too are the two criminals who are crucified with him. One mocks Jesus (v. 39), as do the Jewish leaders and the Roman soldiers (vv. 35–36). They all taunt Jesus, telling him to save himself, but none recognizes him for the Saviour that he is. It is only the other criminal who sees that Jesus can save him, and Jesus assures him that they will be together in paradise. Even as he dies—indeed, because he dies (cf. 22:20)—Jesus is able to save others. The death of this penitent criminal who casts himself on the mercy and love of Jesus is no more the end of his life than is Jesus' death the end of his life. Jesus offers hope and assurance to one whom others have condemned, just as he prays for forgiveness for those who act against him (v. 34). Here we have another place where there are differences in the manuscripts of Luke, but again there are good reasons for treating this verse as part of the authentic text of the Gospel.

How does Jesus' death bring about salvation for others? Luke gives no clear answer, but insists that it does. Luke encourages his readers to focus on the present reality of the salvation that Jesus offers—conveyed here by his words to the criminal—rather than the mechanics of how it comes about. The criminal seeks forgiveness and Jesus' answer offers more than is asked. Jesus' response typifies what he has taught about God—that he longs to answer our prayers (11:5–11; 18:7), that he seeks us when we are lost, and that he runs to meet us when we return to him (15:20–24).

6 ... died, and was buried

Luke is aware of the reports of the great portents that accompanied Jesus' death (darkness for three hours, and the tearing of the temple veil: vv. 44–45) and pointed to its cosmic implications, but his focus is on Jesus' death and the reaction to it of those who were present. Just as Jesus has been composed and in control throughout his passion and trial, so his composure and complete dedication to God remain intact at the moment of his death. Only after he has prayed and entrusted himself to God does Jesus die. The serene and peaceful way in which Jesus 'breathed his last' is in stark contrast not only with the violence of crucifixion but also with the cataclysmic events that precede his death.

At least some of those standing by appreciate the significance of what they witness. Just as Pilate and Herod found Jesus not guilty of the charges brought against him, so now the centurion declares him innocent (v. 47). 'Innocent' is almost certainly how a Gentile audience would have heard the word that the centurion uses, and this translation is supported by the way in which the centurion's declaration of innocence follows those of Pilate and Herod. The word can also be translated 'righteous', however, which is how a Jewish audience may have heard it—and this is how it should probably be translated when used of Jesus at Acts 3:14; 7:52 (see also Isaiah 53:11). Unlike Pilate and Herod, the centurion responds appropriately to Jesus. He stands in a line of those who have recognized God at work in Jesus, so joins them in glorifying God (cf. 2:20; 5:25; 17:15; 18:43).

The response of the crowd is quite different (v. 48). Whether they beat their breasts as a sign of repentance for having been caught up in the events that led to Jesus' death, or simply as an expression of grief at the execution of Jesus (and perhaps the two criminals), is unclear.

The reaction of those who knew Jesus is perhaps more puzzling still. The whole group is said to be standing at a distance (v. 49). Also, whereas both the centurion and the crowd are said to 'see' what took place (vv. 47–48), Luke says that it was only the women from among those who knew Jesus, not all of them, who were 'watching' these things (v. 49). This is clear from the form of the Greek verb translated 'watching'. Later, these women will be eyewitnesses to Jesus' resurrection. For now, however, they watch from a distance. It is as if they are unsure how to react to seeing Jesus on a cross. We, the readers, know what will happen next, but these women and the other acquaintances of Jesus do not. We do well to join with them in their grief and confusion before moving too swiftly to what will happen next. The joy of Easter will be greater if first we watch and mourn with the women, both at the cross (v. 49) and at the tomb (v. 55).

Guidelines

Like the other Gospel writers, Luke goes to great lengths to stress that it was the Jewish authorities, not the Romans, who wanted Jesus killed. Yet he is also aware that Jesus died on a Roman cross, at least ostensibly on a charge of political sedition: 'This is the king of the Jews' (23:38).

This way of presenting the human responsibility for Jesus' death has had different effects at different times and in different places. For Luke's own contemporary followers of Jesus, a small minority struggling to make its way in the Roman empire, it was useful to emphasize that their movement was no threat to imperial order, and that even its founder had not been found guilty of anything by the Roman official under whose authority he was executed. Yet, in other contexts, most notably medieval and modern Europe, where Christians were the dominant majority and Jews a minority, these texts have had an impact that their authors could hardly have foreseen. They were used by some Christians not to show that they were loyal subjects of the political order in which they lived, but to assert that Jews were the killers of Christ and needed to be treated accordingly. Thus, texts written about a Jewish prophet and his followers came to be used to fuel Gentile anti-Semitism.

The fact that the Gospels have been used in this way is one thing; that they *should* be so used is another. Luke is at pains to show that not all Jews rejected Jesus, just as he is at pains to show that it was the will of God that Jesus should die. Pilate, Judas and the Jewish authorities may have played their part, but it was God's will for Jesus to be handed over, so that he might be raised and so that repentance and the forgiveness of sins might be preached in his name. All humans, not just one nation of people, are offered forgiveness. All humans, not just one nation of people, are guilty of sin. All of us are the reason why God sent his Son to live, die and be raised for our salvation.

1 The witness of the women

Luke 24:1–12

Just as some of the women who followed Jesus witnessed to and supported his ministry in Galilee (they remembered his words because they had heard them: vv. 6–9; cf. 8:1–3) and were eyewitnesses to his death and burial (23:49, 55), so now they become the first witnesses to his resurrection (24:10). Their ability to believe what they are told (vv. 8–10), which coheres with what they now remember that Jesus himself had said, overcomes their initial confusion and fear (vv. 4–5).

The women's ability to believe also contrasts strongly with the refusal of the male disciples to believe what they are told (v. 11). Peter's impetuous decision to run to the tomb makes his response to the women's testimony less condescending than that of the other male disciples, but it is by no means clear that Peter yet comes to share their faith. Certainly he sees the tomb empty except for the grave clothes, but Luke describes him as 'amazed' rather than believing (v. 12). Only later, after Jesus has appeared to Peter, does Luke make clear that he now believes; and only then—presumably after they have heard of Jesus' resurrection from Peter rather than from the women—do the other disciples also believe (24:34). The significance of Luke's rebuke of these men, like his commendation of the testimony of the women who have much to teach the other disciples, should not be ignored.

At the heart of this scene are the words of the two men: 'He is not here, but has been raised' (v. 5). Luke claims that it is God who has raised Jesus (in support of the translation 'has been raised' rather than 'is risen', see Acts 2:32; 3:15; 4:10, among others) and has thus vindicated all that Jesus did and said. Yet he also proceeds immediately to show how Jesus' own words have been fulfilled. The two men's invitation to the women to remember Jesus' words is an invitation directed also to us. Just as the women needed to understand their present experience through what Jesus had taught them, so too do we. Just as they needed to learn to serve Jesus where he now was, not in a place he had left, so we need to do the same. The one who raised Jesus and calls us to follow him is the God not of the dead but of the living (v. 5).

2 Jesus in all the scriptures

Luke 24:13–27

Luke's account of Jesus' resurrection moves from the shock of his absence, as experienced by the women at the tomb, to the shock of his presence, as experienced in the upper room. Bridging these two accounts is the story of his appearance on the road to Emmaus. At the empty tomb, the two men had invited the women to remember what Jesus had taught them, and it was as they remembered Jesus' words that they came to understand what had happened. Now Jesus himself teaches two of his disciples, but it is to scripture, not his own teaching, that Jesus refers them.

To which parts of the Jewish scriptures did Jesus point these disciples? This is an obvious question for us to ask, but it may be significant that Luke himself does not address it. Perhaps there are clues in the apostolic preaching and teaching that he presents in Acts (for example, Acts 7; 8:32–35) and in the Jewish scriptures on which his Gospel has already drawn. But there may be good reasons why Luke does not point to particular passages here. First, Luke claims that Jesus refers not just to certain passages but to scripture as a whole. 'Moses and all the prophets' is an inclusive way of referring to Jewish scripture, the Christian Old Testament, and Jesus finds things 'about himself in all the scriptures' (v. 27). Luke's point seems to be that the whole of scripture points to Jesus and to his cross and resurrection, and that the whole pattern of God's activity points to, foreshadows and culminates in the suffering and glorification of his Son. Here in Jesus' selfless self-giving we see what God is truly like and how his purposes for his people and for all the world come to fulfilment. Jesus takes texts with which these disciples are familiar, but shows the disciples how to read them in a different way—to see with fresh eyes what was always there but which they could not see before.

Yet still Cleopas and his companion cannot move from what scripture says to what is happening in their very presence. These disciples have Jesus himself to explain the scriptures to them, but still they cannot see. They continue along the road but they do not recognize their companion. Might this be a second reason why Luke did not spell out which texts Jesus used? Perhaps he wished to suggest that knowledge and understanding of scripture is not in itself a sufficient basis for Christian discipleship, but that following Jesus requires something more—an appreciation of his presence over and above what we gain by reading the Bible. Certainly scripture is of foundational importance for Christian life—but is it all that we need if we are to recognize Jesus' presence with us today?

3 Known in the breaking of the bread

Luke 24:28–35

When, at last, Cleopas and his companion recognize Jesus, it happens unexpectedly. At the table, the penny drops. Jesus' teaching from scripture has prepared the way, but it is when he takes bread, blesses and breaks it and gives it to them that their eyes are opened (vv. 30–31). They recognize their companion and, as soon as they do, he vanishes from their sight. This is the climax of the story—the moment when they recognize Jesus, the moment when they experience for themselves that he is alive and present with them. It is also the moment to which they refer when they rush back to tell the others in Jerusalem: 'Then they told what had happened on the road, and how [Jesus] had been made known to them in the breaking of the bread' (v. 35).

Jesus is known to these two disciples 'in the breaking of the bread'. Not for one moment am I suggesting that Jesus celebrated the Eucharist, but Luke's eucharistic language seems unmistakable and strongly suggestive (v. 30; cf. 22:19; Acts 2:42). Just like us, Christians of Luke's day could not see the risen Christ physically present with them, but we, like them, can have the living Jesus made known to us in the breaking of the bread. Jesus was present throughout the journey to Emmaus, yet Cleopas and his companion could not see him. They experienced his presence in the breaking of the bread, and it was then that everything else fell into place. They recognized him in the breaking of the bread, and it was in the light of this encounter that they realized how their hearts had burned within them when their companion opened the scriptures to them. Their minds had been informed, their hearts had been touched, but they only realized it in the breaking of the bread.

On one level, Luke's story is that of the transformation of two individuals. On another, it is the story of how Christians may still encounter Jesus and learn to see him as more than merely a stranger and fellow traveller, moving from blindness to sight, from despair to delight. The risen Jesus is ascended, but it is this physical absence that allows for his universal presence by his Spirit. In the reading of scripture, and in the breaking of bread, the risen Lord continues to be present, though unseen.

4 Risen flesh and blood

Luke 24:36–49

Luke's story of the risen Jesus' appearance to his disciples takes place on the same day as the preceding account of Jesus' appearance on the road to Emmaus. The similarity between these accounts is seen in the way in which Luke follows the same structure in each. Jesus is not recognized when he appears to his disciples, and they believe only after an extended encounter with Jesus in which he teaches them from the scriptures and remains with them for some sort of meal.

Luke's presentations of the two meal scenes are very different, however. In Emmaus, Jesus disappeared as soon as he shared the bread. In Jerusalem, however, Jesus is seen to eat (v. 43; cf. Acts 1:3; 10:41). He does not share a meal with the disciples, but eats in order to demonstrate that he has been raised bodily from the dead. His invitation to his disciples to look at his hands and his feet is extended in order that they may be sure that this is the same Jesus with whom they travelled to Jerusalem, not a ghost (vv. 37–39). This gets the disciples some of the way (v. 41), but it is through eating in their presence (vv. 41–43) that Jesus is able to assure them that he has been raised. Only then can he move on to explain how his death and resurrection fulfil the scriptures (vv. 44–46).

The first part of Jesus' teaching to the gathered disciples covers similar ground to his teaching on the road to Emmaus (vv. 44–46; cf. vv. 26–27). Now, in the light of their experience, the disciples can remember and understand things that previously they had failed to grasp (cf. 18:31–34). But Jesus' teaching also looks forward to events that are still to come, which will be narrated in Luke's second volume. The consequence of his suffering and resurrection is that repentance and forgiveness of sins are to be proclaimed in his name to all nations (v. 47). Jesus is about to leave his disciples but his promise of power from on high (v. 49) means that those whom he now commissions will not be left alone. God's presence by his Spirit is promised to all Jesus' disciples, as once it had been promised to his mother (1:35). Details from the end of the Gospel echo details from the beginning: God is doing something new, and he promises his Spirit to those who will work with him in fulfilling his will.

5 He ascended into heaven...

Luke 24:50–53

Although it is short, Luke's account of the ascension is the climax of his Gospel. Now Jesus completes the journey that he has been making ever since he set his face to go to Jerusalem (9:51); now he accomplishes his departure (9:31) as he is carried up into heaven (v. 51). Jesus' ascension is presupposed throughout the New Testament, but it is only Luke who offers a narrative account of the ascension as a visible event. Here Luke presents it as having taken place on the same day that Jesus was raised from the dead (see the clear temporal markers at 24:1, 13, 29, 36, 50), so it is the conclusion both of his resurrection appearances to his disciples and of his earthly ministry as a whole. In Acts, however, Luke depicts Jesus' final departure as taking place after 40 days (1:1–11). Thus the ascension helps to provide both a suitable closing for Luke's first volume and a suitable opening for his second (which may go some way towards explaining why Luke appears to place the ascension on a different day in each volume: he is more interested in providing a fitting ending and beginning for each part of his narrative than in presenting a tidy timeline). Jesus' ascension marks the end of one stage in God's plan to bring salvation to all people, as well as the beginning of another.

Luke's record of the apostles actions in volume two is not the start of something completely new but the continuation of what Jesus had already begun.

Jesus blesses his disciples as he withdraws from their presence. It is a gesture of comfort, for he does not leave us alone. Though no longer immediately accessible as he was when Jesus lived among us, yet he is present both in the breaking of the bread and through the power from on high that his Father promised (24:35, 49). Luke ends the first part of his orderly account with Jesus entering into his glory (v. 51; cf. 24:26), but he points ahead to the way in which his followers will be witnesses (24:48) to what Jesus has set in motion. Previously, some of the disciples have seen a glimpse of Jesus' glory (9:32), but only now do the disciples worship Jesus. Only now, after the resurrection, when they see Jesus' glory and regal power in all its fullness, do they finally grasp who Jesus is. Only now do they respond as they should. We who would continue their work do well to worship Jesus with them, and to be continually blessing God (v. 53). This is what those must do who understand that Jesus now reigns as ascended Lord.

6 ... and is seated at the right hand of the Father
Acts 2:14–36

Luke's Gospel ends on a fittingly climactic note. Therefore, readers who do not know that Luke wrote a second volume have no obvious reason to realize that the narrative of Luke leads into the narrative of Acts. Nor do they have reason to be any less satisfied at the end of Luke than they would be at the end of Matthew or John, or one of the longer endings of Mark. Yet none of the Gospels suggests that the story is over, for in different ways each indicates that it will continue in the story of those who continue to follow him even after his resurrection.

Luke points to the future and the story of the Church in two ways. One is Jesus' commissioning of his disciples as his witnesses (Luke 24:48). The other is his instruction that they wait in Jerusalem until he sends upon them what his Father has promised (Luke 24:49). In our final reading, from Acts 2, we see how Jesus' words are fulfilled. A new age has dawned, for God's promised gift of the Spirit is now poured out on all people (vv. 17–21). Thus, the last days—the days in which Luke and his contemporaries were living, and in which we live today—have begun. Jesus' promise to his disciples has been fulfilled, for from his place of exaltation at God's right hand he has poured out the Spirit whose manifestation Peter's audience can both see and hear. Jesus has been raised and, because of this, a whole new range of possibilities has begun. God's Spirit is offered to all people, and all who call on the name of the Lord shall be saved.

Peter's speech begins by explaining the meaning of what the crowd can see and hear. It identifies this event as the fulfilment of scripture, and roots it in the story of Jesus of Nazareth—attested by God, yet rejected and crucified and then raised from the dead (vv. 22–24). All of this, says Peter, was according to God's plan (vv. 23, 31). It means that 'God has made him both Lord and Messiah, this Jesus whom you crucified' (v. 36); 'This Jesus God raised up, and of that all of us are witnesses' (v. 32). Peter moves from proof texts to personal testimony, and draws both on scripture and on his own immediate experience as he witnesses to what God has done in Christ. That is what Christians have always done, and what we are called to continue to do today.

Guidelines

Only when they knew Jesus in the breaking of the bread did Cleopas and his companion understand why their hearts had burned within them. Had they understood before, they would have known Jesus' presence even though they could not see him. Here, as throughout his narrative, Luke writes for people like us. We cannot see Jesus, yet there may be moments when our hearts burn within us on account of the presence of the risen Lord walking with us, calling us to walk with him, and teaching us to see in scripture what we had not seen before. The risen Lord invites us to his table, where we proclaim his death until he comes, and where he invites still others to join with us in receiving all that he longs to give. It is for this reason that we draw near with faith, that we respond to the invitation that he extends.

Perhaps, for us, as for Cleopas and his companion, it is when we encounter the risen Lord in the breaking of the bread that the key is given to understand what the scriptures might say to us today.

FURTHER READING

Commentaries on the Gospel according to Luke:

Luke Timothy Johnson, *The Gospel of Luke*, The Liturgical Press, 1991.

Judith Lieu, *The Gospel of Luke* (Epworth Commentaries), Epworth Press, 1997.

Henry Wansbrough, *Luke* (The People's Bible Commentary), BRF, 1998.

Studies of Luke's thought:

Stephen Barton, *The Spirituality of the Gospels*, SPCK, 1992, ch. 3.

Paul Borgman, *The Way According to Luke: Hearing the Whole Story of Luke–Acts*, Eerdmans, 2006.

Joel Green, *The Theology of the Gospel of Luke*, CUP, 1995.

Christopher Tuckett, *Luke* (T&T Clark Study Guides), Continuum, 2004.

On the passion narratives in all four canonical Gospels:

Henry Wansbrough, *The Passion and Death of Jesus*, DLT, 2003.

ESTHER

Esther is a very unusual biblical book. It stands out from most of the rest of the Bible in that it never mentions God at all. Most of the Old Testament is a story about the history of God's relationship with his people, but this story is only about the people; God does not feature in the narrative. The closest reference to God comes in 4:14, which says that if Esther does not act, 'deliverance will rise for the Jews from another quarter' but she and her family will die.

What is more, many of the characters have dubious morals. It is not only Haman who comes badly out of the story. Ahasuerus is portrayed as a hard-drinking, violent, intolerant king, and even Esther and Mordecai rejoice in the brutal killing of their enemy. The less savoury aspects of this story have led a number of commentators, both Jewish and Christian, to wish that it was not canonical. For example, S. Sandmel, a prominent 20th-century Jewish scholar and rabbi, stated that he would not be at all unhappy if the book of Esther dropped out of the canon. This statement is echoed by many Christian writers, not least Martin Luther, who said that he wished it didn't exist at all.

And yet... the story is immensely popular and forms the foundation for the great celebratory Jewish festival of Purim, when the deliverance of God's people is remembered. The story of Esther may not be the greatest theology of the Old Testament or the most profound ethical teaching; its power lies in the telling of the story of ordinary people (even if one of them is a queen) who have to find great courage in the face of looming disaster. It is a story of people like you and me, and, as a result, its power continues to resonate with us many years after it was written.

The date of the book of Esther is hard to identify but many think it one of the last of the canonical texts to reach its final form (in around 165–140BC). Some, however, think that it finds its origins much earlier than this, in the late 4th century BC.

1 Queen Vashti's downfall

Esther 1:1–22

The opening scene of the story of Esther paints a picture of a state that is morally bankrupt and in need of help. The narrator gives us something of the backdrop of the Persian setting as he sees it, so that we can understand the story of Esther better. This passage has two mini-scenes in it.

The first scene tells us of three lavish banquets. In the first, the king entertains the nobles of the land for six months, followed by a second seven-day banquet for everyone (that is, every man) who lives in the capital. At the same time as this second banquet, Queen Vashti gives a banquet of her own for the women of the city. The narrator makes sure that we appreciate the excess involved in these banquets: their length (vv. 4–5), the demonstration of the wealth and power of the king (v. 4), the decoration of the palace for the event (v. 6), the lavish implements used at the feast (v. 7) and the great amount of alcohol consumed (v. 8).

This first scene leads into the second crucial scene, which gives the immediate backdrop to the choice of Esther to be queen. King Ahasuerus, in the midst of the demonstration of all his wealth and belongings, decides also to show off his wife, but she refuses to come. Vashti stands out in this story as a strong character with a sense of self-respect. The king is asking her to display herself as a concubine might, and she, mindful of who she is, refuses.

The king's response is to make this a matter of state, rather than a personal matter, and calls together his advisers to help him deal with it. Their solution is laden with irony. Their concern is that Vashti's refusal to come before the king will become known throughout the land and challenge the mores of the day. Their solution is laden with irony: they decide that Vashti should no longer be allowed to come before the king (the very thing she had just refused to do) and that this should announced across the land (making sure that everyone hears about it).

So the scene is set for the rest of the story that follows. We know now that the land and its king are corrupted by wealth and excess, that women in the land have no position of respect or power, and that when they attempt to establish some self-respect, they are defeated by the king's closest advisers. Esther is about to enter a situation in which she surely cannot succeed… or can she?

2 Queen Esther's rise

Esther 2:1–18

The second scene of the story sees the king seeking to replace Queen Vashti. The language of verses 1–4 seems to imply that the king regretted what had happened: when his anger died, he thought about Vashti and what had happened to her. Again, in this seemingly innocuous piece of detail, the narrator lays the ground for future events. The king remembered 'what had been decreed against her'. It is almost as though this all-powerful regent is bested and ruled by his advisers. Those who know the story will be reminded of Haman, who tried to best the king as well. The whiff of regret is painted subtly by the author: in his anger, the king set a course of action in progress that he was unable to alter.

The solution to the problem is some kind of ancient beauty contest. As a result, Esther finds herself in the royal harem, undergoing the necessary beauty treatments (twelve months long) before being presented to the king. Again, this scene establishes certain principles that are vital to the rest of the story. We encounter Mordecai, Esther's cousin and guardian, who continues to care for and advise her when she is in the harem. We also discover something about her family. Mordecai's (and, we presume, also Esther's) great-grandfather was one of those who were taken into exile by the Babylonians. Mordecai's and Esther's family, therefore, have been struggling, in the famous words of the psalmist, to 'sing the Lord's song in a foreign land' (Psalm 137:4). This helps us to understand something about the message of the book of Esther. In a way, the book is an exploration—a case study, almost—of how to sing the Lord's song in a strange land.

The other feature that comes out in this chapter is the way in which Esther makes the best of difficult circumstances. The story makes it clear that neither she nor Mordecai had any control about her arrival at the royal palace—the decree went out, so she had to obey—but that once there, she quickly won the favour of Hegai, the eunuch in charge of the harem. In other words, Esther was not just a pretty face! There was something about her that set her apart from the others in the harem.

3 A plot foiled

Esther 2:19–23

The final scene-setting episode of this opening section of the book of Esther concerns possibly the least well-known part of the story. The opening of verse 19 indicates that this event takes place before Esther has been made queen—that is, while the virgins are still being gathered together in the palace. The setting is the king's gate, where Mordecai is to be found. It is not entirely clear from the story why Mordecai is at the king's gate. Two options present themselves.

The first possibility is that, out of concern for Esther's welfare, Mordecai hovered around the king's palace to enable him to see Esther as often as possible. The second (which is more favoured by scholars generally) is that Mordecai had some kind of place in the king's court. The palace gate in the ancient Near East was where officials gathered to undertake the legal business of the kingdom, so 'at the king's gate' became used figuratively for being in the court.

While he is at the palace gate, Mordecai learns of a plot against the king's life. He tells Esther, she tells the king and the plot is averted. The significance of this small episode is twofold. First, it makes clear, yet one more time, the kind of regime in which Esther finds herself—a regime in which the enemies of the king are hung on the gallows. This, added to the other scene-setting episodes, establishes the tension of the narrative from the very start. Esther lives in a morally corrupt, greed-driven society where even the queen can suddenly become the enemy of the king and where enemies are hung on the gallows.

The second significant point of this episode is that Mordecai is demonstrated to be one of the few people of integrity in the story. He seeks to preserve the king's life for no gain to himself: the tip-off is anonymous, and he receives nothing for it. The characters of this story are painted in extreme hues. There are the very good, such as Vashi, Esther and Mordecai; the very bad, such as Haman, Bigthan and Teresh;

and the powerful but neutral, such as Ahasuerus, who seems almost helpless at the hands of the other characters in the narrative.

4 Haman gains power

Esther 3:1–15

The general sense of foreboding engendered by the opening scenes is enhanced by the next event in the story. The opening made it very clear that Mordecai and Esther had decided to keep their identity as Jews hidden (2:10), the implication being that it would be dangerous to reveal their identity. In this episode, however, Mordecai's identity as a Jew is forced from him by the actions of Haman.

One interesting feature of this account is that the ethnic origin of Haman is stated here (v. 1), as is Mordecai's (v. 4). There is a significance in this. Haman's ethnic origin is given as Agagite. Agag was the king of the Amalekites who was defeated by Saul and put to death by Samuel (1 Samuel 15:8, 33). There was an ancient and bitter feud between the Amalekites and the Israelites as a whole, but the Benjaminites in particular, of whom Mordecai was a descendant. The sense of foreboding that has already been established is heightened when we realize that Haman's enmity towards Mordecai is ethnic as well as personal.

The presenting issue for the enmity between Haman and Mordecai, however, is power. The newly promoted Haman expects everyone to bow down to him, but Mordecai's belief in God prevents him from doing so. Haman understands this as a challenge to his power—which indeed it is, though probably not as Haman interprets it. In the introduction, we noted that the book of Esther is a reflection on how to sing the Lord's song in a strange land. Here we find the first of the book's answers to this question.

One of the striking features of the story so far has been Mordecai's desire to blend in with the Persian culture, but here we discover that this is not entirely possible for him. There are occasions when allegiance to God overrides any desire to adapt to the society in which we live. For Mordecai, this is one of those occasions.

Haman's response is a recognition of the fact that Mordecai's refusal to bow down to him comes from his religious allegiance, not from personal enmity, and, on these grounds at least, is logical. If being a Jew means that a person cannot accept Haman's absolute power, then the solution—which the opening scenes of the books lead us to expect—must be to annihilate the Jews.

5 Esther must act

Esther 4:1–17

Mordecai's response to Haman's edict is both anguished and dramatic (v. 1). Although his actions may seem melodramatic to us, they underline the isolation of Esther within the Persian court. Mordecai has to act dramatically because otherwise Esther may not get the message about the importance of what is to take place.

Mordecai wears sackcloth—the traditional garment of mourning—and is thereby denied access to the pleasure-loving court. Nothing is allowed to interrupt the revelling of the court—least of all those in mourning and in fear of their lives. This desire to avoid pain at all costs presents a powerful challenge to our own culture, whose love of pleasure resonates a little with that of the Persian court. The avoidance of pain is a natural reaction and yet, as becomes clear, encourages an environment in which injustice can abound. A culture that refuses to listen to other people's anguish can all too easily become a culture that turns a blind eye to those who cause that anguish.

Despite the fact that Mordecai cannot enter the court, his mourning reaches the ears of Esther and she sends a messenger to enquire about its cause. In the process, the central crisis of the story and Esther's own calling within it becomes clear: she is to try to save her people from annihilation.

The choice she faces is stark: risk death by approaching the king or leave her family (as well as herself, perhaps) to certain death. In the course of Mordecai's challenge to Esther, we encounter (as we noted in the introduction) the closest reference to God in the whole of the book: if Esther does nothing now, the people will be saved but her family might die.

Mordecai's faith is striking: he is in no doubt that God's people will survive, even if he and his family die. This is an oblique reference to the assurance of salvation history. The relationship between God and his people is so strong that the people *will* be saved. It may not be today or tomorrow—it may not even be in the lifetime of the speaker—but one day it will happen.

6 Esther risks her life to save it

Esther 5:1–8

At the end of the previous scene, Esther asked Mordecai to fast day and night for three days before she took her petition to the king (4:16). The timing here is significant. Haman's decree against the Jews went out on the 13th of Nisan (3:12), which is the day before the great Jewish festival of Passover. This whole event, therefore, spans the period of Passover. This adds a resonance to the story: will God intervene in history to save his people as he did in the exodus? Mordecai's prayers fit into this model: the catalyst for the exodus was that God heard the cries of his people. Esther asks Mordecai to send similar cries up to God, and then seeks to be a new Moses for her people, to set them free from oppression.

Esther's solution brings to mind the fate of Vashti. Vashti fell from favour at a royal banquet when she refused to answer the king's summons. Esther, rather boldly, summons the king and Haman to a banquet of her own. In order to do this, however, she must gamble upon the king's mood. The story has already made it very clear that King Ahasuerus has great mood swings, and sees no problem in choosing another wife if the current one displeases him. Esther's decision to stand before him involves huge risk, but it is a risk that pays off and the king grants her a request.

One of the mysteries of the story is why, when promised half the kingdom, Esther does not simply ask for reprieve immediately. The answer probably lies in Haman's power. It would take more than the whim of a king to unseat someone as powerful and determined as Haman.

Guidelines

Some books of the Bible are so rich with theology that their meaning tumbles out as soon as you start reading them. Esther is not one of them: in fact, it is quite the opposite. On first reading, it can appear that the book is little more than a good yarn about a dramatic piece of Jewish history. A closer reading of the text, however, makes this story relevant to each one of our lives. The setting might be light years away from our own but the dilemmas, anxieties and problems faced by the characters are immensely relevant.

The question around which the story revolves is 'How do you live with integrity in a culture driven by pleasure and excess?' The experiences of Mordecai and Esther resonate strongly with those of many people in the 21st century.

The answers given may be a little surprising. We might expect the book to say that we should shun all aspects of such a culture, but it does not. Instead, it seems to suggest that it was fine for Esther to be a Persian queen and Mordecai to be a member of the court—until this life led to a clash of allegiance; only then were hard decisions to be made.

This message is helpful today. How do we live in a world so driven by money and pleasure? The answer may be, 'the same as Mordecai and Esther did' until this world asks us to make a choice between our worship of God and its own principles. At that point, we must stand with integrity and accept the consequences that arise from such a stand.

1 Pride comes before a fall

Esther 5:9—6:11

We saw at the end of last week's readings a chink of hope for Esther as she sought to save her people. Haman, however, was still so powerful that she had to tread carefully. In today's reading we see the seeds of Haman's downfall. The problem with ambition for money and power is that no gain is ever quite enough; the desire to get that bit more money or to wipe out one more opponent seems to take over. This passage demonstrates how driven Haman had become by his own success.

Esther 5:11–13 reports Haman telling his wife and friends how much he has—money, a large family, a high office and prominence second only to the king—but that this is all spoiled by the fact that he saw Mordecai on his way home. Haman's animosity towards Mordecai, which began when Mordecai found himself unable to acknowledge the absolute power of the official, has begun to eat away at him—so much so that he can longer be content with what he does have. The first seed of Haman's downfall, therefore, is sown by his own hatred and anger.

The second seed of destruction, unbeknown to Haman, is sown by the king's memory of Mordecai's virtue. After a sleepless night, the king asks for his court documents to be read and discovers Mordecai's unrewarded act of kindness. Haman, who has just arrived to arrange Mordecai's execution, is tricked by the king into suggesting for Mordecai the honour that Haman would have most liked for himself. This scene is laden with irony: what ought to be Mordecai's worst day turns out to be his best, and what ought to be Haman's best turns out to be his worst!

Lying behind these passages is a sense of God. Again, although God is not mentioned explicitly in the text, we get a sense of God's presence. There are a remarkable number of coincidences in this text: the king cannot sleep and learns of Mordecai's unrewarded actions at the very same time that Haman seeks to bring about his execution, and Haman arrives in the court at the very time that the king wants to ask advice on how to honour his favourite. This number of coincidences suggests what some people call 'God-incidences'—that is, God-inspired fate rather than a random series of actions. Even if God was involved in these events, however, we cannot avoid the conclusion that the real agent of Haman's downfall was, in fact, Haman himself, whose greed and self-serving interest at least contributed to his untimely end later in the story.

2 Haman's downfall arrives

Esther 6:12—7:10

The seeds of Haman's downfall, hinted at in yesterday's readings, begin to sprout and grow in today's readings. When he arrives home from his enforced honouring of Mordecai, in great shame (so much so that he covered his head), Haman's own wife prophesies that his vendetta against Mordecai will prove unsuccessful (6:13). The interesting feature about her words is that she assumes Haman will fall because the Jews are invincible. This picks up the theme of the previous passage, that

God instigates many coincidences that contribute to Haman's undoing. Another interesting feature about 6:12–14 is the contrast between Mordecai and Haman in the reason for their mourning. Mordecai was in mourning (4:1–4) because of the potential loss of his whole people, Haman because of the loss of his power.

Thus, Haman's power is beginning to unravel even before Esther acts. The dramatic climax of the story is reached swiftly in 7:1–10. During the second banquet thrown by Esther, the king repeats his invitation to her to request whatever she wants, up to half of his kingdom. In response, she simply requests her life and the lives of her people. In the lavish and excessive society described by the narrator within the Persian court, the simplicity of this request casts into harsh relief the contrasts of the kingdom. For the privileged, there was the opportunity to ask for and receive untold riches; for others, even their lives were at stake. The character of Esther straddles these worlds. She is invited to ask for wealth but the greatest wealth she can hope for is the lives of her people.

The king's angry reaction seals Haman's fate. In a moment, he falls from being able to do no wrong to being able to do nothing right. Even his desperate attempts to plead to Esther for his life enrage the king still more (7:7–8), and so his fate is sealed. The final twist of irony for Haman is that the gallows prepared for his enemy Mordecai are, in the end, used to finish Haman's life. The significance of the height of the gallows (50 cubits high) is that as well as killing his enemy, Haman also hoped to humiliate him by ensuring that everyone around would see his death. As it happened, however, this shameful death was allotted to Haman instead.

3 The Jews are saved

Esther 8:1–17

Esther 7:1–10 only begins the process of reversal of fortunes. This theme is continued in 8:1–17. The first sign is that, for the first time in the whole story, the king makes his own decision and appoints Mordecai to Haman's old position. The threat to the Jews, however, is not over. It is this that makes clear the true origin of the king's anger. He is not fuelled by anger at an injustice to innocent people but by the thought of losing

45

his beautiful queen. Esther still has to persuade the king to change the edict allowing the extermination of the Jews. Thus it becomes clear that the kingdom swiftly returns to business as usual—the only difference being those who are advising the king.

There remains a problem. Although Haman is no longer alive and seeking the death of the Jewish people, his decree remains in force. One of the features of Persian law, we are told, is that it is irrevocable. Presumably based on the belief that the king is always right, this means that the king cannot simply overturn his previous decree and free the Jews from potential annihilation. Again the king's weak character is highlighted as he turns the whole problem over to Mordecai: 'You may write as you please with regard to the Jews, in the name of the king' (v. 8). In other words, 'You sort out this mess.'

Mordecai's counter-decree perfectly balances and neutralizes the previous one: the Jews are given unlimited powers to 'assemble and defend their lives, to destroy, to kill, and to annihilate any armed force of any people or province that might attack them, with their children and women, and to plunder their goods' (v. 11). In other words, while the decree to annihilate the Jews remains, the Jews can now gather an army of their own people together to defend themselves with impunity. In a single move, therefore, power shifts within the kingdom. The Jews go from a beleaguered, powerless people to a strong group within the nation—so much so, in fact, that people now begin to pretend to be Jews in order to protect themselves (v. 17).

4 The Jews fight back

Esther 9:1–14

One of the intriguing features of this story is that just when you think it has come to an end (for example, in the defeat of Haman, the reward of Mordecai, or the counter-edict of Mordecai), something else happens to take the story on a little. Here we see the actual outcome of the two conflicting edicts of Haman and Mordecai. On the day when those who hate the Jews are hoping to annihilate the people from among them, the Jews manage to fight back and defend themselves.

One of the areas of dispute among scholars when discussing this passage is whether or not the Jewish actions here mark them out as being as bloodthirsty as the Persians. Some argue that this passage presents a massacre of defenceless Gentiles, others that it is simply an act of self-defence. The text seems to point in the second direction and to indicate that the wrath of the Jews fell only on those who sought to kill them: their actions were aimed at defending their own innocent people. This is emphasized by the declaration that they took no plunder (v. 10): the Jews were no marauding mob but a disciplined and defending army. In this passage, the author seems to be highlighting the theme of reversal that has run through the second half of the book. The story began with the dismissal of a queen who would not do what the king want and the description of the power of a man who sought to kill the Jewish people. The end of the story tells of the king doing what Queen Esther wants, of the execution of Haman on the gallows meant for Mordecai, and the victory of the Jewish people where they were expecting defeat and slaughter.

Nevertheless, the principles of the story point up the radical nature of Jesus' ministry in the world. The book of Esther follows entirely the Old Testament principles of defence and restraint. The often-quoted principle from Exodus 21:23–27 is that a life should be taken for a life, an eye for an eye, and so on. The point is that retaliation against one's enemies should be restrained and proportionate—which is exactly as the Jews behave here. The message of Jesus, however, is much more radical than this. Not only should we not slaughter our enemies indiscriminately; we should turn the other cheek and love our enemies (Matthew 5:38–39, 44). This command is even more challenging than the restraint displayed in this passage.

5 Purim is instituted

Esther 9:15–32

One of the most challenging features of this part of the story are the events depicted in verses 15–16. So far in the story, the narrator appears to have gone out of his way to demonstrate the restrained and proportionate response of the Jews, but here something different seems to take place. Haman's edict limited the slaughter of the Jews to a single day, and Mordecai's counter-edict limited the defence of the Jews to the same day (13 Adar), but here, on 14 Adar, the text recounts that in Susa an additional 300 people were killed. This apparent flouting of the edict, continuing the slaughter on a second day, is at first glance disturbing. It seems to overturn the image of restraint and proportion painted in yesterday's reading.

The reason soon becomes clear, however, in verses 17–32. The author now proceeds to tell us about the festival of Purim, which was celebrated when the book of Esther was written and continues to be one of the most important Jewish festivals today. Purim originated, the author tells us, on the days after the Jews' great act of self-defence, when they rested and feasted to celebrate their reprieve. The feast was instituted by Mordecai, who sent a letter to all the Jews in the region commanding them to celebrate their reprieve; by the people themselves, who took upon themselves the responsibility for continuing the tradition; and by Esther, who sent a letter confirming Mordecai's command.

The importance of this passage is that it tells us something of why the author has written the story at all. It is clear that the narrator of the account is responding to questions within his own community about why they celebrate Purim and why they celebrate it on a different day than other Jews. Verse 24 tells us that the feast celebrates their reprieve from annihilation (and not their victory over their enemies); like the Passover, it reminds them of salvation.

The question of when they celebrate it brings us back to the second day of fighting mentioned in verses 15–16. At the time when the book of Esther was written, the feast of Purim seems to have been celebrated on two different days: in Susa on 15 Adar and elsewhere on the 14th. Verses 15–16 are intended to explain this difference. The explanation they give is that the fighting went on a day longer in Susa than elsewhere, so the celebration began a day later. To our eyes, this is an incomplete and unsatisfactory explanation, but it seems to have been important for the author's original audience.

6 Mordecai celebrated

The end of the story of Esther focuses once more upon Mordecai and stands in great contrast to the opening scene. The beginning of the story painted a picture of the corruption, excess and injustice of the court of Ahasuerus. This epilogue describes a very different scene. The person in power is now Mordecai, and he is as powerful as Haman was previously, being second in line to the king. He is recorded as being powerful and popular, seeking the good of his people and the welfare of his descendants. How great a contrast this is to the start of the book: at last there is the sense of justice and goodness prevailing in the land.

And yet… a lurking sense of unease is suggested by the words of this passage. Mordecai is popular among the Jews, and he oversees the welfare of *his* descendants. Are the other inhabitants of Persia well off under Mordecai, or are the Jews alone treated well? There is no real answer to this question. The book does not seek to tell us; nor, indeed, is it the purpose of the author, whose concern is the welfare of the book's original audience, not its current one.

The ending of the book of Esther stresses the theme that has been bubbling beneath the surface throughout the second half of the narrative—that of reversal. In the beginning of the story, the Jews were oppressed and in fear of their lives; at the end, their welfare is uppermost. At the start, Mordecai was powerless and fearful; at the end, he is powerful and just. Although God does not appear in the book, the footprints of God are stamped throughout the story. Themes of redemption, freedom from oppression and justice illustrate the reign of God, even if God himself does not appear. It is in this that we begin to see the purpose of God's absence from the pages of the story: God may be absent but God's people are not. The principles of God's rule in the world can be carried out in the person of those whom he calls. Despite Esther's and Mordecai's apparent unwillingness to get involved at first, their courage, sense of justice and compassion for their people achieved what God does elsewhere in the Old Testament. In other words, God was present in the form of the people who carried out the principles of God's kingdom on earth.

Guidelines

The book of Esther stresses a profound truth in an unusual form. We all know that part of God's covenant with us is that we will seek to carry out God's will on earth—expressed in the New Testament in the words of the Lord's Prayer, 'Your will be done, on earth as it is in heaven' (Matthew 6:10). Normally, this is expressed in relation to God's own action in the world; here, the focus is entirely upon human action. Esther and Mordecai must act as God desires, even without the obvious intervention of God. In reality, then, the book of Esther reflects life as many of us experience it. Although we often feel the presence of God in our midst, it can feel as though we have to act 'on our own' to carry out God's will in the world.

The book of Esther tells the story of what can happen when remarkable people of God do take on the responsibility to act as God requires. Like many people before and since, Esther and Mordecai changed the world in which they lived; they brought salvation, justice and peace to their people. There have been many like Esther and Mordecai in the history of the people of God: we don't have to think hard before bringing to mind Mother Teresa, Desmond Tutu and others who have acted courageously to change their worlds. What this story reminds us is that we, too, are called to act in this way. It may be dangerous, as Esther and Mordecai discovered, but if we succeed we bring the world one step closer to heaven. The challenge to each one of us as we read this book is whether or not we will accept this calling and live our lives accordingly.

PRAYER

The call to pray, and to prayer, may be welcomed and enjoyed, or entered into with some hesitation. This may depend upon the prayer itself, whether a general prayer of intercession or the personal seeking of God's direction in life. Prayer is both corporate and personal. There is a call to come to offer prayer within a gathered worshipping community, in a small prayer group, or alone.

The Bible is full of words of wisdom and insight as to how the people of God have sought out the presence of God in prayer; how they have heard God speak, often unexpectedly, often not welcomed by them. There may have been a degree of hesitation about following all that God asked of them, but there was no hesitation in the way they expressed their feelings and emotions, as we see in the Psalms.

Throughout the centuries of the Old and New Testament periods, prayer was the means of being in communication and relationship with God. It remains so today. Yet we cannot limit prayer, to define it simply through words that are spoken, whether these are words of a formal prayer or words that come straight from the heart. Prayer is multifaceted and includes much more—silence, music, art, poetry, the natural world, tears, laughter. Prayer is whatever draws us closer to the God who calls us, and here, perhaps, we enter the realm of personal prayer rather than that which may be viewed as corporate prayer.

Over the next two weeks, we will be looking at various passages from the Bible to see what can be discovered to provide inspiration for our prayer. The call to pray is the call of God to us to come and pray for ourselves and for the rest of the world, and to deepen the relationship we have with God.

All Bible quotations are taken from the New Revised Standard Version.

1 Early in the morning?

Mark 1:35; Romans 8:26–27

These two short readings set into place two important foundation stones for our journey of prayer.

The first foundation stone: the Gospel tells us that Jesus 'got up and went out to a deserted place, and there he prayed'. It's reassuring to know that Jesus needed to escape from the crowds and go somewhere quiet to pray and be with God. It's not always easy to pray quietly in a house with other people around. Jesus went out in the early morning before the sun was up and the household woke up, and before the day broke with busyness and noise.

There is no record of how Jesus prayed or what he said—just that he prayed. For Jesus, there was the inner call to be quiet with God, maybe to find peace, refreshment and strength for the journey ahead. If Jesus needed this, then how much more do we?

This verse asks us to think about the pattern of our own personal prayer life. The time we give to God in prayer for our own personal journey, as well as prayers for world issues and people we know, will depend upon the commitments we have.

What time of the day do you read *Guidelines*? Is this a time you also spend in quiet prayer? Is it as important to you to pray for your own journey of faith, to deepen your relationship with God, as to pray for others?

The second foundation stone: when we encounter in our lives pain, distress, fear, anguish, extreme joy and happiness, for example, then we may discover that words fail us, that we are unable to find the words to express all we need to say. Yet the words we look for are not as important as the feelings and the emotions that seek expression. How easy or difficult is it to bring your feelings and emotions into your prayer life?

Paul writes, seemingly from experience, that when we cannot or don't know how to pray, then the 'Spirit intercedes with sighs too deep for words' (v. 26). God understands. However cryptic and muddled our thoughts may be, God knows what it is that we are saying.

When we come to pray, we come as we are and from the context of that particular moment. To know this can give us a sense of freedom, a freedom that enables us to pray in the quiet and from the heart.

2 The Lord's Prayer

Luke 11:1–4

Luke shows a deep interest in prayer throughout his Gospel—prayer as a requisite for a rightful relationship with God. He portrays Jesus as praying for the people around him, using parables to teach about prayer as well as personally encouraging the disciples to pray.

Matthew places his version of the Lord's Prayer in the early days of Jesus' ministry, within the Sermon on the Mount (6:9–13). The time-setting is different in Luke, with the prayer being slightly shorter and placed alongside the teaching of a parable on being persistent: pray, pray and pray again!

The disciples must have noticed the effect upon Jesus after a time of prayer, and so they come to Jesus and ask him, 'Lord, teach us to pray' (v. 1). Jesus responds by giving to them a prayer that we still pray today. The Lord's Prayer, though, is not so much a 'how to pray' as a 'what to pray'. Knowing that they had witnessed him retreating to a quiet place, perhaps Jesus thought the disciples knew 'how to' pray but were uncertain about what they should pray about.

The prayer he gives is one that encompasses every aspect of our lives—from intercession to confession, the local to the cosmic, for all that is needed for the present day and the following day. It is a prayer in which we pray for ourselves as well as our neighbour, a prayer that invites us to be active participants in God's kingdom. It is prayer that reflects the gospel message as proclaimed by Jesus, a prayer that will never become old-fashioned or redundant.

The Lord's Prayer is probably the most well known of all prayers, but, however familiar it is, it retains a powerful dynamism that continues to reach into the fast-changing world of today. Our basic needs may be the same as those of the disciples of Jesus, but the context in which we pray will be different. As we pray the prayer today, it reflects the needs of ourselves and of the world in this present moment.

Is the Lord's Prayer a prayer you pray each day? How do you pray the

Lord's Prayer? One way is to separate the lines or phrases of the prayer, then to take each one as a 'heading' out of which personal and intercessory prayer can evolve.

3 Making prayer personal

Isaiah 43:1–7

These verses from Isaiah are set during the time of Israel's exile. The Israelites have become an insignificant and voiceless people, yet, as the verses unfold, they speak not only of hope and restoration, but of the fact that these people are loved and precious to God. How comfortable are you with the thought of being loved and precious to God?

Verses 1–4 tell us what God will do for his people. There is hope given to those in captivity: 'Do not fear, for I have redeemed you'—or, more simply, 'I am with you', as verse 5 tells us. Verses 6 and 7 move the people into the future: they will be free because they are the sons and daughters of God. These are the words of the God who is with them, watching over them, guarding them, loving them. Who is the God you pray to? How would you describe God?

In the Old Testament, God is personal only in the sense of being 'their God'—the God of the nation. Yet a time will come when all will know God for themselves, and in Jesus we discover this further revelation of God, not to the nation but to individuals. From Pentecost onwards, this revelation becomes more evident, as through the Spirit a personal relationship is offered. It is a relationship that needs to be received and nurtured into greater depth as we come to know for ourselves that we are loved and precious to God.

Whenever the prophets spoke the words of God to the people, it was usually to the nation as a whole. In this passage, the words are for the individual. It opens with a reference to Israel, but soon moves to the personal: 'I have called you by name, you are mine' (v. 1) There is a reminder of the covenant relationship and the fact that every person has a part to play in the ongoing history of creation, as God's chosen people. At the end of verse 7, assurance and hope are given once more, with the reminder that we are created to give glory to God, corporately and personally.

Read through these verses, but place your own name within the passage so it becomes personal to you. Hear God speak your name, call you by your own name, and say to you, 'You are precious in my sight, and honoured, and I love you' (v. 4). How easy or difficult, comfortable or uncomfortable, do you find using these words as a personal prayer?

4 A right relationship

Luke 18:9–13

What constitutes being in a right relationship with God? What is required of us to build up a right relationship with God? We look to the parable of the Pharisee and the tax collector, which could have as a subtitle the saying, 'Pride comes before a fall'!

The parable is addressed to those who either opposed the gospel message or had not yet fully understood the teaching of Jesus. Two very different people come to the temple to pray. Although in a public place, the prayer of the parable is a personal offering to God.

Biblically, to 'pray' can refer to the corporate as well as the private sphere of prayer and worship. The parable is placed within the context of a morning or evening service of atonement, so others are present and it would be normal for individuals to offer their own prayers during the service (see Kenneth E. Bailey, *Poet and Peasant; and Through Peasant Eyes*, Eerdmans, 1997). When in church, how easy do you, or would you, find it to bring your own personal thoughts to God in prayer?

The Pharisee and the tax collector may have been a part of the worship community, yet they both stand away from everyone else; they each stand alone, and for very different reasons. The Pharisee keeps his distance in a display of his own self-worth: he stands aloof, proud, and speaks of his own achievements. The tax collector keeps his distance from a sense of unworthiness and sinfulness, and beats his chest in contrition as he comes to seek the mercy of God.

Who is in a right relationship with God? The Pharisee had kept the commandments, and could be seen as being in a right relationship with God. Yet there is something vital missing, and this we find in the tax collector—humility and honesty.

With our closest friends and those we love, if a relationship is to grow and deepen it has to be built upon love, trust and honesty. Likewise, for our relationship with God to grow, the heart has to be open to the loving touch of God. In our prayer, we can then come humbly before God to express with honesty our deepest thoughts and feelings, which we may find difficult to share with others.

How would you describe your relationship with God? How easy or difficult do you find it to be totally honest with God in your times of prayer?

5 'Come'

Matthew 14:22–33

'Come' is a very simple word, yet at the same time complex. It embraces a multitude of possible responses and reactions—mainly to accept or not to accept. How many questions raced through Peter's mind, I wonder, in those seconds after Jesus said 'Come', before he responded by stepping out on to the water?

To set the passage in context, it follows the feeding of the five thousand. Jesus shows his power over creation, doing what the disciples knew, through their reading of the scriptures, God had done in the past (see Exodus 13:21–22; 16:1—17:6; Joshua 3:14–17; 1 Kings 17:1–16). Now, Jesus retreats to the mountain and the disciples head for their boat and set sail. They have witnessed a miracle, but in the early hours they are tired, cold and afraid.

For Peter, as for the other disciples, this was to be a time of testing. Peter expresses the paradox of faith and belief—having faith and lacking faith. Yet through this experience comes the confession of faith: 'Truly you are the Son of God' (v. 33). They have journeyed through their doubts and fears to reach a deeper faith-awareness of the God who calls them to 'come'.

As for the disciples, so too for us. Our times of prayer and study, like all of our life experiences, shape who we are and play a part in the way we relate and respond to God. To question and doubt can deepen our understanding of the God who calls us to 'come', to help us take that next step on the road of discipleship. Has there been a time, or times, when you have heard God call you to 'come'? Where has that call led you?

This passage is one that can be prayed imaginatively, to weave into it your own fears and doubts. Find somewhere quiet to sit and read through the passage a few times. In your own way, imagine the scene—the boat, the disciples and what they are doing. Place yourself with them; sense the darkness, the water, the wind, the movement of the waves; see Jesus walking towards you, hear him call your name and say 'Do not be afraid. Come.' What do you do? When you are with Jesus, what do you both say? At the end of the prayer time, reflect on your thoughts and feelings and perhaps note anything you want to remember.

6 Offering praise to God

1 Chronicles 29:10–19

To offer praise to God is a constituent part of communal worship, and will also find its expression within our private prayer. What does it mean to you to offer praise to God? Praise embraces giving thanks, the joyful awareness of God's presence and love, expressions of awe and wonder, and much more. In our hymns and songs, the words of the prayers, the gestures that we make in worship, we give praise to God. In your time of private prayer, what proportion of that time is given to praise and how is it offered?

There are verses within this passage that will be familiar. These words have transcended the centuries to find a place within the liturgy (at the offertory) of the Anglican Holy Communion service. Words that gave praise to God then still give praise to God today. This reminds us of the spiritual heritage that infuses our own faith and prayer, which can be traced back into the lives of the people of the Old Testament.

Throughout his prayer, David is aware of the ancestry of his faith: 'O Lord, the God of Abraham, Isaac, and Israel' (v. 18). He looks to those who have gone before, recognizing the transitory nature of human life, and the God who is 'for ever and ever' (v. 10)—God of the past, present and future. This is the God we can come to in prayer, to find strength and hope amid an ever-changing world.

David's prayer comes in response to the freewill offerings that will provide for the building of the temple. In the midst of all those gathered, David praises God for everything with which they have been blessed.

Towards the end of the prayer, he includes a personal request that Solomon may be enabled for his work of building the temple. In all that he says, he affirms his understanding and belief of the power of God.

This passage is a prayer letter of praise in which David acknowledges God as the central focus of all that is in his life. Look at the way David expresses his praise and thanksgiving: what words would you use? If you were to write a prayer letter to God, what would you give thanks to God for? David included a request for Solomon: out of the people you know, who would you include and why?

Guidelines

In a poem entitled 'Prayer', the poet-priest George Herbert (1593–1633) writes:

> *The soul in paraphrase, heart in pilgrimage*
> *The Christian plummet sounding heaven and earth.*

These two lines speak about prayer that encompasses the everyday routine of life, yet holds something of the infinite and divine—a linking of 'heaven and earth'. On this day, as we participate in services and acts of worship, we join our personal prayers to those offered corporately. On one level, our prayerful participation remains personal, but on another level we are reminded that we are not alone on our pilgrim journey.

It is 'the soul in paraphrase' that seeks to express our inner thoughts and feelings, and now widens to embrace the issues and concerns of the wider world. It is 'the heart in pilgrimage' continuing its journey with and to God. Where, in your heart, will your prayerful pilgrimage lead you today?

1 Freedom of speech

Psalm 8

We begin this week by coming to the hymn book, or the prayer book, of the Hebrew scriptures—the Psalms. Psalm 8 is a psalm of praise, wonder and awe that gives glory to the God of creation. It speaks of our human smallness in relation to the infinite love and majesty of God. In comparison with some of the other psalms, this may be called a 'gentle psalm'. The psalmists were not afraid, as sometimes we may be, of coming to God and saying exactly how they felt and what they expected God to do for them.

To read and pray the psalms is to find images and words that can bring us to a deeper relationship with God through an honesty of expression, in and through the circumstances of life in which we find ourselves. As Gordon Mursell says, 'The psalms were written out of first-hand experience, in a world where violent oppression and arbitrary, motiveless tragedy caused people to constantly challenge and doubt received orthodox wisdom: in other words, in a world remarkably like ours' (*Out of the Deep*, DLT, 1994, p. 45).

Because of this, the psalms transcend the centuries, passing with ease from the ancient to the modern, and to the postmodern world—making them relevant for us today. Regardless of the century, feelings and emotions need to be expressed, and we can find comfort in knowing that others have found the words we ourselves need and maybe cannot find.

The psalms record far more than a people's experience of life and faith. They are more than merely words of prayer, whether praise or lament. The psalmists express deep inner struggles as they try to make sense of events beyond their control; they wrestle with God in the words that they use to find a way of living in the world. The psalms are prayers of protest, hope, fear, anger, doubt, praise, faith and so much more. They are prayers that bring into the open our true inner self in a call for transformation.

Do the psalms have a place in your prayer life? How do you feel about the difficult verses—for example, those that talk about revenge on enemies? Do you read them or ignore them? Which of the psalms are your favourites, and why?

2 God's dream for our lives

Jeremiah 29:10–14

'I know the plans I have for you... plans for your welfare and not for harm' (v. 11). These are words from God of hope and expectation—and also of something yet to be discovered. At the same time, there is the sense that this plan, or dream, is already set into place and all that is needed is for it to be found.

To set the scene, the people of Judah have been taken into exile in Babylon, and it is left to the prophet Jeremiah to keep in contact with them. He writes words of encouragement to help them settle in the communities in which they now find themselves. Few of the original exiles would live to return to their own land, and many who would return would be too young to remember anything but life in Babylon.

In these verses, the hope for the future is twofold. Firstly (vv. 11–12), hope and restoration will come to them, but will come only through the grace of God. Secondly (vv. 13–14), if hope and restoration are to be realized, it is up to the people to seek out the presence of God in their lives. God is willing to be found, perhaps for those with the eyes to see and those with the eyes to look within.

Through these verses, we can come not only to find words of hope that can reach into whatever situation we are in, but also to dream our own dreams. It's important to have a dream, however impossible it may seem to be in reality. It is also important to discover *God's* dream or plan for us. His dream or plan will mean that we live out our lives in faith and can fulfil all the potential that lies within.

Has there been a time in your life when you felt you were in a place of 'exile', uncertain about the right direction to take for your future? What dream do you think God has for your life—a dream that will bring you out of exile and into the place where you are called to be? Spend some time dreaming your own dream—the dream that could happen, and your wildest and most impossible dream.

3 Rejoice in the Lord!

Philippians 4:4–7

From the dreams of yesterday we come to a more realistic understanding of joy, and a joy that is founded upon faith in God. This joy is not dependent upon what we may be doing or feeling, but is a deep inner joy, rooted in the knowledge of God in our lives.

To the people of Philippi, the call to the whole congregation is to 'rejoice in the Lord' (v. 4), the Lord who is with them in the persecution they are facing. They are to seek a faith that has substance, not just a thin surface veneer. Only with a deep faith and awareness of God will they have the confidence to be faithful. Paul also reminds them that, whatever they may be facing personally, they still need to look out to the wider world and not to be focused totally on their own worries.

When we are in the midst of apparent darkness and face one problem after another, it may not seem too easy to follow Paul's advice. It may be difficult to pray as well. How do we view the world as a whole when we have difficulty coping with the world that makes up our own daily lives?

On the surface it would seem that worry, anxiety, fear, doubt and uncertainty are not allowed. There are countless places in the Bible where God says, 'Do not be afraid; do not worry or be anxious', yet God knows that built into our human nature is the tendency to worry, to be uncertain. These verses go beyond the surface into the depths of who we are, to the God who, with peace, is with us even if are not aware of it.

To remember the peace of God, the peace 'which surpasses all understanding' (v. 7), is to come to rest in the presence of God, to rejoice in being with God. It also may mean that, first, we come to offload all our inner pains, angers and frustrations.

Has there been a time when you have felt a deep peace within, that is God-given? Has there been a time when you have felt the deep need to rejoice in prayer before God? How does it feel to remember this? Does the remembering help you to journey through other, or present, difficult situations?

4 Let the light shine through

Ezekiel 36:23–27

At the end of verse 23 we read, '… when through you I display my holiness before their eyes'. These are thought-provoking words; they are also challenging words to ponder over in a time of quiet prayer. What does it mean that God will display his holiness through us, making that holiness visible to others?

In these verses we see Ezekiel anticipating all that will be fulfilled in the New Testament. He writes of the time when, God says, 'a new spirit I will put within you' (v. 26), a time of inner cleansing and transformation.

As a start, new hope is offered to the exiled nation, but they need to believe in God and give to him due honour and worship. The Israelites have a part to play, to seek out once more the way of the God of their ancestors. The more they focus their lives on God, the more they will come to discover the image of God within, and so make visible the holiness of God.

In Jesus, with his promise of the coming of the Holy Spirit, we move closer to this time of inner transformation. It is a time of renewed awareness of the God who calls out to us—yet, as with the people of Israel in exile, God awaits for our response, our turning to him.

For us, transformation comes through the work of the Holy Spirit as we seek to deepen our relationship with God. The more we become in tune with God and who we are as people, the deeper will be the awareness of God's abiding holiness within us, which we need to make visible to the wider world. Even in our brokenness, God's light can shine through us.

Imagine a candle and how much light its flame gives to a dark room. Its light changes everything: it gives shape, colour and presence. John O'Donohue writes, 'Light is the greatest unnoticed force of transfiguration in the world: it literally alters everything it touches and through colour dresses nature to delight, befriend, inspire and shelter us' (*Divine Beauty*, Bantam Books, 2003, p. 92). The light we are to show is the light of God's love and holiness, which is to reach out and touch every aspect of our lives—a light to make the truth of Jesus visible.

How does the light of God's holiness shine through you?

5 Always and everywhere

1 Thessalonians 5:16–24

At the beginning of today's reading, we find three exhortations given to us by Paul. We are to rejoice, to be at prayer continually, and to give thanks to God (vv. 16–18). This may be far easier to say or read than to do. Yet Paul is concerned that only if we look to our inner and spiritual self will true and right relationships be fostered and lived out in the wider community.

Paul's solution to a better outward way of life is to concentrate on God and on prayer—to pray always and everywhere. For Paul, prayer is an essential element of everyday life if a deep and deepening relationship with God is being sought, and that prayer can be expressed in a multitude of ways. We thought yesterday about allowing the inner light of God to shine through us; today, we see how we may be enabled to do so, through the call to pray continually (v. 17). This is the interweaving of prayer and the spiritual with our day-to-day lives, the unceasing prayer of lives lived in faith.

Again, this may appear at first to be the impossible dream. Yet, to pray unceasingly does not mean that we are continually offering verbal prayer to God. It is more about the whole of our being having at its foundation a faith in the triune God. Because we do not constantly and consciously think about those we know and love, it doesn't mean that we have forgotten them. They remain with us in love, and it is likewise in our relationship with God.

To pray unceasingly is something that transcends praying with words alone. Prayer becomes a part of our inner feelings and emotions; it holds us in our busy times and in times of quietness; it strengthens us in times of need, and expresses in many ways our faith and beliefs.

How much time each day, or each week, do you spend in prayer? How easy or difficult is it to add up the minutes you spend in prayer? How many different ways of praying do you use through the course of a week? For example, you might include silence, written prayer, confession, thanksgiving, praise, intercession, a quick 'arrow prayer', or praying through creation. How creative are you in prayer? For example, do you draw, or paint, use music and dance, or write your own prayer poetry?

6 To dwell in Christ

Today we read Paul's prayer to the Ephesians. It is a prayer of great depth and intensity, a prayer from the heart. He begins by saying, 'I bow my knees before the Father' (v. 14), which expresses powerfully the personal feeling within Paul that lies behind this prayer. To kneel was not common practice for the Jews, who stood to pray, and so to kneel emphasizes a deep emotion that needed to be brought before God.

In churches today, kneeling seems to have gone out of fashion. Do you kneel or sit to pray in church, and why? In times of private prayer, what is the most comfortable posture for you—for example, to sit in a chair or on the floor, to lie down, to walk around—and why?

Within Paul's prayer, all people are included in the relationship with God, as one family where all are equal. Paul prays that this family of faith may be enabled and equipped with all that is necessary for them to be followers of Jesus, which comes through the indwelling of the Holy Spirit.

He prays for the gifts of the Spirit to be upon them. He prays for wisdom and understanding, not only an intellectual understanding of all they have learnt about Jesus, but an intimate awareness, through personal experience, of God's presence in their lives. To know God's love for themselves is what Paul seeks for those he prays for. This is a prayer that transcends time and reaches out into our lives today. It is a prayer that is also for our own strengthening of faith, that Christ may be within our hearts, as Paul prayed he would be within the hearts of the Ephesians.

The prayer ends with the church and with Jesus. The church gathers the people in to worship, then sends them out into the world to proclaim the love of God—but, Paul says, this can only happen through Christ Jesus. Through him, the inward journey to the God who dwells within them then leads the way outwards, equipping them to go out as disciples in Jesus' name.

Is there someone you know for whom you could pray this prayer? Which gifts of the Spirit are needed in your life at this moment?

Guidelines

Is personal prayer for our personal journey and relationship with God the most neglected of prayers? As we come to understand ourselves, our own feelings and emotions, at the same time we discover something more of God. As we become more open and aware of our own self, we may be surprised at the many and varied ways in which we encounter God, and not only in a specific time of prayer.

How has God surprised you this week? Have you discovered anything more about yourself through this week?

FURTHER READING

Gordon Mursell, *Praying in Exile*, DLT, 2005.

John Pritchard, *How to Pray: A Practical Handbook*, SPCK, 2002.

Nicola Slee, *Praying Like a Woman*, SPCK, 2004.

You may also wish to consult books by Margaret Silf and Joyce Rupp.

LIFE IN THE WILDERNESS

Wilderness and the experience of wild places is a key theme in the Bible and particularly in the Old Testament. One scholar has described it as 'the single most informative experience in the creation of the Jewish people' (Carol Ochs) and another (Ulrich Mauser) says that without it the development of religion in the Old Testament would be unintelligible.

In the Old Testament, the wilderness theme comes in both background and narrative in the exodus, in Elijah, in the exile, even in Job and Jonah. In the New Testament, it features prominently for John the Baptist and Jesus. As a personal encounter, it surfaces in one character after another, from Hagar to Paul and all stations in between, in the prophets (often as a spiritual metaphor) and as a physical phenomenon in the Writings, especially the Psalms.

In presentation and interpretation, it is multifaceted. One day the wilderness is negative, a hostile environment, provoking fear. Another day it is a place of hope and encouragement as the voice of God penetrates the horror—a veritable expression of grace as the wilderness purifies and the experience transforms. Ultimately it is an expression of God himself, the Alpha and the Omega, creation in Genesis and fulfilment in Revelation, to be treated with awe and respect.

In the first week, we concentrate on some of those people and personal experiences mentioned above. We examine a number of stories in which the wilderness provides a backcloth to a series of human experiences in which individuals had an encounter with God, and we explore a variety of different emotions with varying consequences.

Week two tackles broader attitudes and concepts, with reference to the impact of biblical wilderness on contemporary issues relating to the environment. We look at wilderness to appreciate the wonder and diversity of the wholeness of God's creation, in some cases through the eyes of biblical writers as well as characters, and always with one eye at least on our own situation as we try to appreciate God's wilderness in the 21st century.

John Muir, often described as one of the greatest naturalists of all time, and founder of the National Parks in the USA, was second to none in his admiration and exploration of wild places. He was no biblical scholar, but much of what he wrote chimes in with and enlightens biblical comment on the same subject. For this reason, we shall occasionally doff our hat to Muir as we move through the second week.

In twelve days, of course, it is impossible to explore the whole range of interpretation of the wilderness concept. All I can do is to throw out a line here and there, focus on a few incidents, explore them, and so encourage the reader to find similar ideas in other places.

Wilderness as a human experience

1 A vale of tears

Genesis 16:1–6; 21:8–19

After Genesis 1—11, Hagar is the first person to receive a theophany. The wilderness is at the heart of her story, which falls into two Acts. In Act 1, Sarah fails to live up to her good intentions in allowing Abraham to have children by her handmaid and is consumed with envy once the child is born. Life for Hagar becomes intolerable and she runs away into the wilderness. In Act 2, after the birth of Isaac, Sarah's jealousy grows. She calls on Abraham to get rid of both Hagar and her son, and this time Hagar is driven into the wilderness.

Notice the difference: not much had changed in Abraham's household and the wilderness was the same wilderness, but for Hagar it was very different. In Act 1 Hagar chose to go, albeit under pressure. In Act 2, Hagar had no choice. Trevor Dennis focuses the difference by moving the spotlight from the human experience to the divine response, inviting us to look at the 'God who sees' (Act 1) and the 'God who saves' (Act 2).

In Act 1, God's response is to tell Hagar to pull herself together, lift herself out of the wilderness, go back and try again. He has other ideas for her. She needs to think of hope, the future and her potential. But how does that happen? Not because of anything Hagar does but because of what God does. *He* sees *her*—and before she sees him. Wilderness is not the place where she finds God. It is in her moment of extreme distress that God finds her. Her salvation lies only in her capacity to respond, and that comes when she feels noticed.

In Act 2, the 'God who sees' becomes the 'God who saves'. This time, it does depend on Hagar's initiative. Ishmael is dying of hunger and thirst. Before long, she will follow him. All they need to survive is water, but this is wilderness. The water is there, but she doesn't see it. Only when she is so desperate that she picks Ishmael up and gives him a big hug, creating genuine warmth and affection in the wilderness, does she suddenly become aware of a resource that had been there all the time. She had to spot it, and she only found it when she 'found' someone else in the wilderness and responded to him.

2 A place of commitment

Exodus 3:1–12

There are several angles to this story. First, we see Moses the man of privilege. He may not have been the only Hebrew babe who was rescued at birth, but he is the only one we know about and possibly the only one to have been saved by the royal court. Doubtless he grew up with the idea that he was different, and possibly special—maybe also with the feeling that he owed something to society. But which society? With a foot in each of two worlds, he lives in the tension between loyalty to his roots and to his adoptive family, not to mention the material comforts that go with the latter.

Second, there is Moses the man of action. Whoever he is, wherever he is, he cannot stand around and do nothing if he sees injustice. There's no theory, no lectures, no waiting for someone else to do something; he gets stuck in with both hands.

Third, we have Moses the runner. Now he really knows who he is, who he belongs to, who are his friends and who are his enemies. His upbringing as a royal prince is not going to save him and, unable to face the consequences, he runs away into the wilderness and sits down by a well. He responds positively to the sufferings of some women who have come to draw water and are being ill-treated by some shepherds—and ends up marrying one of them.

Thus were sown the seeds that, years later, produced Moses the deliverer: this was the beginning of his spiritual pilgrimage. He became a deserted character who found himself in the desert—older and wiser; more rational and conciliatory, perhaps, but even more determined not to give up until the job was done.

Only imagination and speculation will help to elucidate what it was about the wilderness and the burning bush that brought about the transformation. Perhaps he came to the long-term realization of what it meant to be an alien in a foreign land. Perhaps the quietness, the loneliness, even the isolation, left him with lots of time to think. Perhaps there was a sense of wonder at what he had found and the desire to share it with others. But all the emotion and enthusiasm he could command were not enough without the harsh reality of thought and argument as he worked out the practicalities. Life in the wilderness is like that: the desert is not a place to run to unless you are prepared for a new call and a renewed commitment.

3 A place of redirection

1 Kings 19:11–18

After an extraordinary victory over the prophets of Baal on Mount Carmel, here we have Elijah, like many before him, fleeing for his life—first to Beersheba and then, all alone, a further day's journey into the wilderness. Jezebel was never likely to find him there. Moses's burning bush has become Elijah's broom tree—similar but different. The bush was a beginning; the tree, Elijah hoped, would be the end (v. 4). But he was wrong. As with Hagar, God had other ideas and the wilderness turned out to be a place of redirection.

First, God gets under Elijah's skin. The prophet may say he wants to give up because he is finished, but he doesn't really, and when he is nudged to return to life, to eat and drink, he shows no hesitation. The wilderness is not a dying place: it is a place where life is constantly refreshed and renewed. Unlike bricks and mortar and all the products of human effort, wilderness has a capacity to renew itself. Block it in one place, and it will go in a different direction. Cut it back and you strengthen the resolve. Wipe huge chunks out with machines or natural disasters, then leave it alone, and its inner life breaks through.

That renewal doesn't happen to order, though, never in quite the way you might expect and rarely to replicate precisely what was there before. This is what Elijah had to learn. Here was not the strong wind splitting the mountains and breaking the rocks—the familiar God of power and might, enforcing his will and smashing everything that stands in his way to smithereens; not the earthquake, drawing on hidden and uncontrollable forces to change the face of the landscape; not the fire, wiping out everything that had gone before to make way for a totally new beginning—but the silence.

The silence of the wilderness, especially at night or if you are alone, can be far more terrifying than even the threat of a Jezebel. It can concentrate the mind and touch the depths, and, as one door closes (so quietly that you hardly notice) you realize, like Elijah did, that there is another door you had never even noticed, which is about to open.

In the depths of the wilderness, where you think you know all the ways in which you might expect God to come—forget them. This is the place and the moment to listen for the still, small voice you have never heard before.

4 A place of discipline

Jonah 2:1–9; 4:6–11

Jonah's story hardly looks like a wilderness experience but, for the Jews, the dividing line between uninviting dry desert and a nasty wet ocean was a narrow one. Both suggested fear and anxiety, to which the ocean added extremes of unpredictability. They didn't like the ocean. From time immemorial they had hated it, possibly because they had never had to cope with it, or possibly because of their experiences in crossing the Red Sea and the Jordan—and always lurking in the background was that mythical monster of the deep (Leviathan or Behemoth), believed to have been defeated by God at creation but never far from their consciousness. The sea was wilderness at its worst.

The psalm in Jonah 2 is probably best read as an act of thanksgiving for when the ordeal was over, rather than a *cri de coeur* from down under. Traditionally, to be in the wilderness is to be cut off from God (vv. 3–6a).

After his experience, Jonah comes to see it as the prerequisite to finding God. Of course, he knew God all along. If he didn't, he would never have had the problem in the first place. What he didn't know was how limited his understanding of God could be.

Before, he simply could not believe that God would want him to go to Nineveh. He knew them: they were a bad lot. They would give him a rough ride and he would achieve nothing. Anywhere, even Tarshish, was a better proposition. So when he is forced to go to Nineveh and the citizens respond positively, he is angry. Their repentance may be what God wanted, but it is not what Jonah wanted. God may be generous but Jonah isn't. He knows their repentance won't last.

Unable to transfer the generosity of a loving God to himself, in chapter 4 he tries to transfer his anger against God, by venting his wrath on a sympathetic bush which has given him protection from the heat but failed to survive more than a night. In expressing that anger, he opens the door to God, who gives him the spiritual insight of a lifetime.

Slowly and painfully, Jonah finds a bigger God than he ever imagined. God's domain stretches so much further than Jonah ever contemplated. Every bit of wildness—Jonah, Nineveh, the bush, the ocean, the big fish, the mariners and even the god of the mariners whose name we are never even told—all are his. All are in his care.

5 A place of new birth

Matthew 3:1–11

If, to some, the wilderness was an affliction to be avoided, to John the Baptist it was a blessing to be grasped. From the very beginning, he arrives on the scene as a wilderness character—a loner. The Greek word for 'wild honey' (arros) literally means 'belonging to the field' and, alongside locusts, camel's hair and a leather belt, it suggests an ascetic. John would stand out as a wilderness character wherever he was— independent, a man of strong opinions, all black and white with no grey. The axe goes right to the root of the tree as he chops down everything that has gone before. Nothing from the past is capable of dealing with the present situation. With a tough message, he needs a tough pulpit and an audience brave enough, strong enough and in the right mood to go where they can get it. His presence in the wilderness is no accident. It is the necessary backcloth to everything he has to say.

Yet John's wilderness is neither dry nor barren. There is water in abundance for those prepared to respond. Whether he offers a foretaste or reflection of the early Essene community, which lived on the shores of the Dead Sea and is often associated with the Dead Sea Scrolls, we cannot say, but the similarities cannot be dismissed. John's emphasis is not on what wilderness can do for an individual but on the capacity of the wilderness to touch whole communities. Whole groups and communities can be revived, and the water of baptism is the sign and symbol.

John's preaching is a message for people consigned to the wilderness of life—for people on the margins, from one who lives on the margins. It is a message for people whose driving force is not the desire to be 'number one', people who have come to see that recognizing the light and pointing to the light can sometimes be more valuable than striving to be that light. Therein lies the hope that dispels despair, but it is a hope that springs only from a true recognition of the reality of the wilderness. When that happens, we have neither a return to the old nor even a reconstruction of the old, but a renewal of the old—the same roots but blossoming in a different way.

6 A place of testing

Matthew 3:13—4:16

Wilderness, for Jesus, has many sides. Having experienced the waters of renewal in the baptism by John, his next encounter was to test the reality of that renewal. His wilderness experience proper began with 40 days and nights of questioning and self-examination. The questions that bugged him were the ones that bug most of us, most of our life.

'Should I turn these stones into bread?' There are situations of extremism—times when common sense has to prevail, times when even the most rigid of rules have to be broken or principles modified. But there are also times when somebody has to hold the line, when quick and easy solutions are not necessarily the right ones. How are we to know when to accept and when to reject those solutions?

'Should I jump from the temple?' Promotion, publicity and PR all have their place, but at what point do they cease to be an integral and necessary part of the message and become, instead, a spectacle that distorts the message?

'Can I offer this kind of worship?' Of course there are patterns of worship that people find helpful and satisfying, and there seems little point in patterns of liturgical correctness that serve no purpose for anyone. But where do you draw the line between adapting where necessary to meet people's basic needs, and settling for the satisfaction of adoring crowds by turning worship into entertainment? No shepherd wants to stuff his sheep with the unsuitable or the indigestible, but if the hungry sheep look up and are not fed, then they have a very poor shepherd.

Jesus was not the first or the last to be driven into the wilderness, either to wrestle with these questions or because other people thought he had got things wrong. Nor does his experience give us much guidance for any particular situation we may face. What it does say, though, is that we have to face the same wilderness. His wilderness is our wilderness and, like him, we have to work out the answers for ourselves.

Once Jesus had settled these issues, he saw his ministry in terms of ministry to the wilderness people, whether it was the demon-possessed and others who were banished from society, or simply hungry crowds who followed him there (Matthew 4:24–25). Then it was back to the wilderness again—choosing isolation on the mountaintop (5:1) to evaluate what he had done, to charge his batteries and to prepare for the next battle.

Guidelines
- If every bit of creation is God's concern (as the story of Jonah tells us), where have we been missing him? When we find him, whom should we tell?
- If recognizing the light is so important, make a short list of people and groups not normally seen as 'disciples' but who seem to you to be pointers to the work and will of God. Share them with your friends and work out what you have been missing.
- If one of the readings this week has helped you to identify and recognize a wilderness moment of your own, read that Bible

passage again. How does your experience help you to understand the passage? How does the passage help you to see your own situation more clearly?

Creation as an expression of God

1 God's good creation

Genesis 1:24–31; 9:8–10

The creation story sets the scene. God created the heavens and the earth with (in Genesis 1) humankind as the crown of creation. God's blessing involved being fruitful and multiplying, with dominance over all other living creatures, and the human race found little difficulty in deciding what was intended. As a few human beings became more enlightened, the idea emerged that dominion did not mean 'control for the benefit of the human race' but 'control for the benefit of the whole created order'. All the same, neither scholars nor readers of the Bible ever doubted that it put human beings in the driving seat. Then, more recently, came the realization that God had never meant human beings to control the rest of creation for their own advantage. Somebody spotted a 'correction line', which had not been given the attention it deserved.

God's covenant with Noah recognizes human weakness—'the inclination of the human heart is evil' (8:21)—resulting in a new covenant (the 'cosmic covenant'), this time not just with humankind but 'with every living creature' (9:10). Everything has its place—which is not the same as saying that everything has its uses. The whole of creation is to be protected. In these times of climate change, dwindling energy resources and other concerns about ecology and the environment, this emphasis on protection is finding a new audience—and it has several aspects.

One day, when I was at school, a classmate brought in a tiny toy dog with fine string running through its limbs. When you pressed the bottom to ease some of the strings, the dog collapsed into all kinds of funny shapes. We had never seen one before and it became the wonder for a day. Then somebody suggested showing it to the head, a dour scientific character. 'No,' said another. 'He'll just look at it and say, "Hm. But what does it *do*?" and it doesn't *do*—it *is*.' John Muir once complained that people were always asking 'What are rattlesnakes good for?' as if nothing had a right to exist unless it did something for human beings. He thought it a mistake to assume that 'our ways are God's ways' and wondered why we could not simply allow things to be and exist in God's eyes for their own sakes.

Next time you wander on the hills, in the country or through the forests, try focusing attention on something that, on the surface, has no use at all. See if you can find ways of enjoying and appreciating it for its own sake.

2 God delights in his wilderness

Psalm 104

The NRSV (in some editions) suggests reading this psalm alongside Genesis 1, so try imagining it to be a record of what God felt and said to himself at the end of those first seven days. What do you think might have given him most pleasure? What might have worried him? And what might he say if he was 'rewriting' the psalm today?

If you find it an overlong passage, try reading it aloud. Instead of stopping and pondering over every line, read it quickly and let it wash over you. If you are musical, try to hear and feel the music rather than intellectualize the content. When you have more time, go back and focus on a few verses that have a special appeal for you.

Notice the different impressions of God on which the psalmist focuses.

- The invisible God: not the God you see but the God you know by what he does (vv. 3–4).
- The creator God, whom all nature has learnt to respect, and whose boundaries nature honours (vv. 7–9).
- The caring God, who creates one part of nature to give a service readily to others (vv. 10–16).
- The orderly God, who allocates each part of nature to its own place (vv. 18–23).

Even Leviathan (that monster of the deep who lost out in his battle with Baal and who features elsewhere in the Psalms as one over whom God has total control: 74:13–14) appears here (v. 26) and in Job (41:5) almost as God's plaything, and certainly as one whom God formed.

This is the God to whom the whole of creation, inanimate as well as animate, relates. All creation knows its master as it discovers the hand that feeds it.

As a boy, Muir loved intricate machinery with all the parts working together towards a desired end. Not surprisingly, therefore, he saw the whole of creation as a collection of fragments each complete in themselves, yet all the time revealing itself in different ways, shaping and reshaping itself with the intricacy of complex machinery. This is perhaps what led him to say, 'When we try to pick out anything by itself we find it hitched to everything else in the universe.'

This wilderness was the place where Muir first found God. The psalmist seems to have had a similar experience.

3 Wilderness as threat

Numbers 20:1–13

When ecologists, environmentalists, gardeners and nature lovers are getting all sentimental about wild places, it is important to remember that for many people (possibly for all of us at times) wilderness suggests threat and danger. Wolves do not regularly lie down with lambs. Not everyone can eat and be satisfied. Water shortages can happen in the most surprising places. At such times, many people, like the Israelites, see the difficulties as an adequate reason for rejecting God altogether and turning to other sources of help. Even the faithful ask 'why?' and do not always come up with an answer.

In the incident described by Numbers 20, just what happened is shrouded in mystery, but clearly the water was never far away and there was no real threat to life or limb. The problem lay not so much in the wilderness as in the mixture of impatience and lack of trust suffered by the people, while the solution came from one who was prepared to hope against hope, to trust when all else failed and at the time to explore even the most unprepossessing places and methods to achieve what was needed.

The story also introduces us to another facet of the God of the wilderness: his commitment to his people and his capacity to care for them in every way. He is not one to lead his people up a gum tree, to inflict unnecessary hardship or to neglect them at their point of greatest need, but some circumstances call for patient waiting. This is the case even when we walk in pleasanter places, but patience is hardest when life is toughest.

Instead of complaining, therefore, we might reassure ourselves by spotting the manifold ways in which nature shows herself to be a good mother. Muir reminds us how she 'sees well to the clothing of her many bairns', citing birds with feathers, beetles with shining jackets and bears with shaggy furs, thinly clad animals for the tropics and warmly clothed animals for the Arctic, the squirrel with socks and mittens and a tail broad enough for a blanket, not to mention the mole 'living always in the dark and in the dirt, yet as clean as the otter'.

God's wilderness caters for each according to its kind and for all according to their need. We do not find God in the wilderness until we find ourselves there. Then we find both him and ourselves in a new way.

4 On the move

Numbers 33:1–37

This chapter reads like a tourist's brochure, though hardly one likely to sell many tickets. You can stop reading as soon as you have had enough! The places are not particularly significant but, if you are not averse to writing in your Bible, underline the words 'set out', 'camped', 'turned back' and 'went'.

Franziska Bark notes that the people of Israel were always on the move but never arrived. Deuteronomy ends with the people on the threshold: fulfilment must wait until the book of Joshua. The promise of Canaan may have got them moving, but the arrival was not the sole aim and purpose. This is not the same as saying that to travel is better than to arrive, rather that, for the Jews, their life was in the wandering.

In the context of the journey of life, therefore, the wilderness is a place of constant change and adjustment. Volcanoes explode and pour out their lava. Mountains and seas rise and fall. Ice caps melt and then freeze up again, not necessarily in a generation but over thousands of years—because wilderness follows God's time and God's time is eternity. Wilderness life is not something we go through to get somewhere else, but rather the veritable cauldron in which life is lived.

Contrast this attitude with the frustrations we endure in all sorts of ways because we focus on the objective, the arrival, yet 'never get there'. Where are we going? Where do we expect to get to? And what would we do if we did arrive? Arriving at goals, achieving targets, has its place, but it is not necessarily the 'god' that many politicians, business people and even preachers would have us believe. In many situations, it might be better to void the frustrations and tensions by changing the focus—learning to make the most of where we are.

In some respects, Jews have been better at this than Christians, perhaps because of their history, perhaps because they have had to be. Towards the end of *Fiddler on the Roof*, when the village of Anatevye has been destroyed, they have lost pretty well everything they had and are to become refugees once again, one of the characters says, 'Anatevye was never all that wonderful anyway.' This is not exactly 'tomorrow to fresh pastures new' but a recognition that the 'now' is what matters.

5 God's grace and glory

Job 40:15–24; 41:12–34

The story of Job is well known. His life is in turmoil. Step by step he has lost just about everything he has—possessions, health, friends and family. Few readers could claim such a catalogue of horrors, yet in lesser ways most readers will not find it difficult to identify with his feelings and his basic question about God.

There are many ways (not mutually exclusive) of putting the question. Why me? Why suffering? Why suffering for good people? And for Job, who never claims that he is perfect or even suggests that a modicum of suffering as a corrective or chastisement may be out of place, why suffering so disproportionate to his deserts? It is not only unbelievers or those on the fringe of the church who bridle as they ask the question. Believers at the heart of the church go to their minister or father confessor and ask the same.

Such answers as there are seem, at first glance, to be like those given by politicians who either never hear the question or deliberately use it to explain their own position. In this case, God seems to be telling Job either that he is asking the wrong question or that, if he really wants an answer, he is looking in the wrong place. He needs to start somewhere else. But where? The wilderness; earth; the whole created order.

To the Israelites, God and nature (including the earth of which humankind is part) are not two separate entities, and the created order *in toto* is not a single entity but a process, always dependent on the Creator who sustains life. So understanding God and the way in which he works requires us to understand nature, for it is through nature that we find him. Listening for the voice of God means listening to the voice of the earth (see Dell on Job 28 in *The Earth Bible* vol. 3). For Job and for us, this calls for a new humility.

Notice, too, the contrast between these passages (where human beings are largely ignored in the scheme of things) and traditional interpretations of Genesis 1 (where humans are the crown of creation). Job's cosmos is not to be anthropocentric, and God's primary occupation is monitoring the mysteries of the creation (Habel, *The Earth Bible* vol. 3, p. 74). That very factor leaves Job (and us) with a new set of questions to think about.

6 Renewal in God's way

Isaiah 35

This is the great chapter of wilderness renewal, but before we rush to embrace it we need to be clear that renewal in God's way may not be quite the same as renewal in our way, which too often means little more than restoration.

We have to begin, as Isaiah 35 begins, with the recognition that some things are not right—or at least not as we would expect them to be. There is wilderness and dry land—but there is an expectation that all dry land should produce something. We expect it to blossom and give joy and pleasure. So also with people. Weak hands and feeble knees have a right to strength. Those who live in fear surely need help to overcome their fears. Who would not give sight to the blind or hearing to the deaf if it were within their power? All of this can be achieved when we begin to enjoy God's renewal as the waters wash over the wilderness and bring it to life.

But the blossoming wilderness is not necessarily the same thing as the cultivated wilderness. The crab apple does not have to become a Golden Delicious; it can remain a crab apple. The desert may rejoice and blossom 'like the crocus' (vv. 1–2) but not every plant is going to look like a crocus or the desert become a field of crocuses. Great as it may seem to achieve sight for the blind (v. 5), we need to be prepared for the fact that they may not see as we see: the perceptions of the blind often far outclass those of the visually sighted. Lame people who leap 'like a deer' (v. 6) may not look exactly like people who leap with all their faculties, as we discover when people with severe physical limitations play tennis or climb the Munros.

Renewal in God's way means coming to terms with people and the created order as it is, and not necessarily as we imagine it is or as we would like it to be. It means acknowledging that God knows best: only when we are prepared to talk his talk do we qualify to walk his walk (v. 8), share in his joy in his creation and enjoy the benefits (vv. 9–10).

Guidelines
- Make a collection (or perhaps just a list) of things that appear to have no use whatsoever for human beings. Then try to see them with the eye of God who created them and learn to appreciate them for their own sake, or devote a study group to thinking about such objects and bring specimens.
- Reflect (alone or in a group) on the message of Isaiah 35 in terms of current discussions on the renewal of energy. To what extent are we committed to inherited forms of energy and to what extent is the renewal of energy leading us to think about whether God has something entirely new to put before us.

FURTHER READING

Franziska Bark, 'Time and Torah', in *Judaism*, vol. 49, no. 3 (Issue 195, Summer 2000), pp. 259–68.

Robert Barry Leal, *Wilderness in the Bible: Toward a Theology of Wilderness*, Peter Lang, 2004.

Terry L. Burden, *The Kerygma of the Wilderness Traditions in the Hebrew Bible*, Peter Lang, 1994.

Trevor Dennis, *The Book of Books: The Bible Retold*, Lion Hudson, 2003.

Norman C. Habel (and others), *The Earth Bible* (six volumes), Sheffield Academic Press, 2000–01.

THE ROAD TO CRUCIFIXION

Some church buildings and Christian traditions honour the Stations of the Cross—stopping points along the way to Calvary. In these Holy Week readings, we linger at seven stopping points in Luke's narrative of the tragic conclusion to Jesus' earthly life and ministry (chs. 21—24). Each is central to Luke's climactic account; each rich in history and theology, inspiration and challenge. The notes have been written using the New International Version of the Bible.

Alert readers will notice that 'The road to crucifixion' breaks all the rules by presenting a Bible passage with notes on the seventh day rather than a 'Guidelines' section. Because Easter Day is always a Sunday, our pattern means that we never read the resurrection narratives on Easter Day, which seems a shame. Therefore, for this year only, we will.

1 The end of the temple

Luke 21:5–37

We begin with the temple, one of the wonders of the ancient world (Mark 13:1). Rebuilt by Zerubbabel (see Ezra) and enlarged by Herod the Great (19BC–AD63), the temple had 40-foot marble columns and golden vines 'with grape clusters as tall as a man'. As Josephus, the Jewish historian, wrote in his *Wars of the Jews*, 'The Temple appeared to strangers, when they were at a distance, like a mountain covered with snow, for as to those parts of it that were not gilt, they were exceedingly white.' Jesus' reference to destroying this temple (see John 2:19) must have seemed risible, but his eyes were looking to other things, as Luke discerns. He looked forward to the temple's destruction in AD70, when Jerusalem itself would be ransacked (vv. 6, 24). He looked to the 'day of the Lord' (Isaiah 13:9, Joel 2:1), when 'nation will rise against nation, and kingdom against kingdom', which his Jewish contemporaries linked to the beginning of the perfect age to come (vv. 10–11, 25–26). He looked to his disciples' future persecution (vv. 12–19) and to his own second coming, when God's plan would ultimately be fulfilled (vv. 29–33). All this he saw, as Luke's rich writing captures. This is the vast historical canvas on which Luke depicts the final events of Jesus' life, for his death is set against history and eternity, as pivotal to God's salvation plan.

Jesus' teaching here is honest, direct, comforting and confrontative: 'Be careful' (v. 34); 'Be always on the watch, and pray that you may be able to escape all that is about to happen, and that you may be able to stand before the Son of Man' (v. 36). This first 'station' reminds us that Jesus confronts religious securities and historical realities. He takes the long view, speaks God's word and comforts God's people. At the start of this Holy Week, these truths should amaze us more than religious architecture, military might, world leaders or human folly. But do they?

2 The malicious meeting

Luke 22:1–6

From the broad sweep of history we turn to Jesus' biography, from God's eternal plan to human sin and jealousy. Our second stopping point is that seedy meeting room where 'the chief priests and teachers of the law… looking for some way to get rid of Jesus' (v. 2) conspired with duplicitous Judas to 'hand Jesus over' (v. 6). The dark foreboding of Luke 21:5–38 becomes here more pointed and more personal. Judas is tempted to betray his friend and succumbs; the high priestly party, previously hiding behind Pharisee opposition to Jesus, now takes the initiative. It makes painful reading. As theological and historical orientation to the deeper reason for Jesus' death, the story could not be more relevant.

What happened in that malicious meeting room is well known; what history records, we experience each day. Vested interest secured by political compromise, envy raging against its rival, financial advantage ignoring the human cost, religiosity exposed by genuine faith—this is the stuff of life. The 'crowd', often more in touch with integrity than individuals or leaders are, is here feared and avoided (v. 6). This is a harsh mirror on human fallibility. No wonder Luke invokes Satan as an actor in this drama (v. 3). Satan twists Judas' perception of Jesus. He surely savoured the authorities' 'delight' when Judas approached, and aided when Judas sought 'an opportunity to hand Jesus over' (vv. 5–6). Not all evil is Satan's dirty handiwork but to deny that he has a part, or to say that no act warrants his name, is sub-Christian or unbiblical.

We should avoid making the actions of Judas or the religious leaders irreducibly personal. That is the path of prejudice and pride. Rather, we should learn from them as types of people and practices, as commentaries on the person we see in the mirror. Holy Week causes us to descend into the deep dungeon of human depravity, not to leave us there but to illuminate more brightly the sin from which Christ saves. As Graham Greene wrote so pertinently in *The Power and the Glory*, 'It was for this world that Christ died. The more evil you saw and heard around you, the greater the glory lay around the death. It was easy to die for what was good or beautiful… it needed a God to die for the half-hearted and the corrupt'. Amazing?

3 The fellowship room

Luke 22:7–38

Preparations to celebrate the day of Unleavened Bread extend beyond the day itself, as Luke suggests here. This passage describes Jesus' characteristically detailed planning and the third stopping place in Holy Week. Now we are in that upper room, a fellowship room, to which Jesus and his disciples withdraw. A habitual practice here takes on an exceptional character as we physically leave the temple crowds and religious authorities and enter the private, spiritual space inhabited by Jesus and his closest followers. But we do not leave sin outside that inner circle. Amid the intimacy and withdrawal, friendship and commitment, we find disloyalty and jealousy, false hopes and proud bombast, which destroy religious faith and communities then as now.

Luke continues to weave together skilfully history, theology, biography and comment. Along with the practical preparations for the meal (v. 12), Jesus is preparing for his death and ultimate return (vv. 14–20). Paralleling Judas' betrayal (vv. 21– 22) is the covert competitiveness of the other disciples (vv. 24–25). Jesus' symbolic enactment in bread, wine and word ('I have eagerly desired to eat this Passover with you before I suffer', v. 15), stands in stark contrast to Judas' action, to the disciples' argument and to Simon Peter's shallow self-centredness (vv. 31–38). The consequence of this careful interplay of themes and personalities is that Jesus does not face his trial alone; in reality the disciples are themselves already judged in the light of Jesus' life and love. Those who endure will indeed 'sit on thrones, judging the twelve tribes of Israel' (v. 30), but we wonder if this ramshackle crew will ever attain that honour. They fall far short here. Yet the death Jesus will die is for such as these, for the likes of you and me.

To linger in the fellowship room today is to confront the temptations that test and try every Christian ministry and every Christian fellowship. We should take comfort in the knowledge that our sins are not unique, but we should grieve that we know no better. Perhaps we have fallen into the trap of thinking that preparing the fellowship room obediently (as if laying the table for Communion) is sufficient an act of piety and loyalty. Luke shows how far from adequate that good but limited task really is if it is divorced from the spirit of sacrificial love that inspired the first Lord's supper, the love that he intends always to shape Communion.

4 'The lonely garden'

Luke 22:39–53

Our fourth stopping place is Gethsemane. The disciples are physically present but, as the narrative makes clear, effectively absent in Jesus' hour of need (vv. 40, 45). The spotlight is on Jesus. The teacher of the crowds and author of history, the object of Judas' betrayal and of the disciples' devotion, faces the darkness alone. He knows this place well (v. 39). The garden and experience are not new to him. He has prayed fervently, questioned deeply, struggled vocationally, prepared mentally, many times alone before. This does not lessen his struggle; it enriches it, for his life was a series of difficult, deliberate decisions (of the kind, perhaps, that we too readily avoid). The disciples' lethargy adds to his burden: they succumb to temptations that he resists, and fail in the combat he must win. He pleads, negotiates and struggles with his Father's will (v. 42). Though alone physically, he is ministered to spiritually (v. 43), but his agony persists. His lonely prayer is disturbed by the least welcome intrusion—an armed guard, come to arrest him (v. 47). In dark times, even prayer is disturbed.

Luke's ancient text captures remarkably the atmosphere and psychological torment of Jesus' predicament, betrayal and arrest. Through vivid symbols (the 'drops of blood', v. 44) and evocative images (the cutting off of the servant's ear, v. 50), we are drawn into this harrowing tale. But Jesus' charisma is palpable. To those who come to arrest him, he coolly replies, 'Am I leading a rebellion, that you have come with swords and clubs?' (v. 52). His deliberate vulnerability ('Every day I was with you in the temple courts') contrasts starkly with the planned violence of his opponents ('But this is your hour—when darkness reigns', v. 53).

The fourth stopping place is a turbulent, violent place. The death throes of human sin and institutional power are felt in Jesus' anguish. He is not only fighting himself: he is contending with evil, the evil that motivated Judas, seduced Peter and inspired the authorities, that would all too soon shape the decision of the Roman court and would be finally eradicated only at the end of time. The rugged truthfulness in Jesus' honest prayer to his Father and controlled reaction to his arrest in Gethsemane are reminders of the best weapons we can use in our struggle with self and sin, day by day. But will we learn?

5 The courtroom drama

Luke 22:66—23:49

Commentary on Luke's narrative feels redundant. What more can we say? At every level the story is compelling. We are in a courtroom now, both on earth and in heaven. Jesus is tried and condemned, on earth for (putative) blasphemy, in heaven for (human) sin. Luke's narrative theology is remarkable. He captures Jesus' loss of control in a blur of people and places, conversations and outbursts; for Jesus' crisis (just as our crises do) snatched control from his hands. In contrast, Luke keeps a firm grip on the storyline, and in it he hides theology. This is no disordered, rambling narrative. It has a deep inner unity. The authorities intend Jesus' death, but so does he; their intention is a savage act of naked power, his a willing act of sacrificial love. The motives differ; the ends agree. 'Crucifixion!' to Jesus and the authorities is a shout of triumph.

En route, Peter denies and soldiers scourge (see 22:54–65). Then Pilate and Herod cross-examine, the 'chief priests and teachers of the law' accuse, the 'crowds' crow, Barabbas walks free, and Simon shoulders Jesus' burden. It is a crowded, busy canvas that Luke depicts. Yet the background is clear: God's eternal plan and final judgment, Judas' betrayal and human villainy, the beauty and power of disrupted fellowship, the wonder of Jesus' courage and love. This is the context of Jesus' death.

The reader is also on trial, however, cross-examined by events and by Jesus. 'There they crucified him' (23:33): we cannot read without regret. We feel our complicity, for here is no accident or myth, heroism or masochism, but the deep indictment of human sin. We are culpable; God's verdict stands; prophecies are fulfilled and promises made, and we are the problem that required this solution. The only Son dies in our place, the righteous Judge is unjustly condemned, the true King is brutally overthrown, the Creator is killed, and all for love's sake and ours. With Luther, we see here 'God's strange wisdom', acting 'under its opposites', revealing his glory through shame, his power through weak-ness, his life through death, his victory through defeat, and all *for us*. The means and ends should silence us. In Luke's controlled narrative (mirroring God's deliberate plan), nothing is amiss. Through cruelty, compassion triumphs, and grace pours from the torn body of our perfect representative, Jesus Christ. This is the court's judgment. Do we believe it?

6 The silent grave

Luke 23:50–56

'There was a man named Joseph' (v. 50)—another of those key figures named by the early church (compare John 1:6). After the turbulence of Friday comes the tranquillity of Holy Saturday. Our stopping place is a graveyard—an odd place to linger, perhaps, though many do, for peace, perspective, comfort and grief. In the silence of a graveyard, death sheds light on life. This graveyard is a rocky place; hewn graves house chambers and channels for shrouded bodies. In the light of a new day a new reality begins to dawn.

Luke invites us to ponder Joseph's integrity, to let his character ('a good and upright man', v. 50) illuminate ours. Though 'a member of the Council', he has not participated in the actions of the Sanhedrin. His mind is on higher things than politics and cruelty ('he was waiting for the kingdom of God', v. 51). He looks to do the honourable thing, risking his reputation in the process. He asks Pilate for Jesus' body and takes it to a new grave (vv. 52–53). Because of the sabbath, he delays final burial preparations, allowing 'the women who had come with Jesus' (and followed Joseph, v. 55) time to prepare the customary spices and burial cloths. Not until the sabbath is ended will their devoted work be done.

It is a silent space that we enter today. Shadowy figures move through mists of uncertainty now that Jesus is dead. Luke captures well the empty listlessness of the newly bereaved—numb, confused, shocked, searching for something but unsure what. The solid figure of Joseph dispels some uncertainty. He is an impressive transitional figure between the old order of Jewish ritual and new order of resurrection faith. By his impartial action we know that Jesus is dead (no swooning, body-swapping or deception possible now). By his good deed, the evil of the previous day is further exposed. In honouring tradition and the dead, one good man gives another a decent burial. The spiritual continuity between Jesus and Joseph adds beauty to this graveyard garden. Even in death, grace is evident. The pressure of divine love moves a good person in a ghastly situation towards a good end (see Romans 8:28). Though death is silent, it is not empty. God shares the grave and graveyard. Many testify to the presence of the angel who, like Joseph, redeems tragedy, and the light that dawns when the darkness of death descends.

7 The terrifying tomb

Luke 24:1–12

We should rejoice and tremble today, lest we dishonour Jesus' resurrection. Today history, reality, ethics, faith, relationships, hope and life are redefined. Today Jesus is renamed Son of God and Saviour, Lord and Christ (Romans 1:4). Today death's power is broken, sin and sickness are weakened, and hope is anchored in history. No wonder angels (v. 4), fear (v. 5) and disbelief (v. 11) are part of Luke's Easter story.

Easter is, of course, one event in two parts: it is Good Friday and Easter Day. To view it otherwise risks faithless pessimism (facing death without hope), or naïve triumphalism (seeking glory without pain). Balanced Christianity holds both together, however tough life and faith may be. Christian faith that proclaims 'He is risen from the dead!' faces reality, names pain and embraces hope.

Despite Jesus' predictions (Mark 8:31), nothing could have prepared the disciples for what happened. Luke's historical urgency (Luke 1:1–4; Acts 1:1–4) addresses the event's implausibility. The disciples' disbelief is understandable. Here is no myth, alibi, deception, feeling or joke. In every sense the resurrection is deeply true, spiritually and historically. God's 'possibility' trumps every human 'impossibility' in giving life to the dead. And if so, what else might he do? Jesus' resurrection makes life both more and less certain. We linger at the empty tomb to allow the horror of Good Friday and glory of Easter Day to invade our souls and disrupt our world. In *every* event and consequence that we reckon inevitable, resurrection renders it no longer so. To the fatalist, pessimist or determinist, it says, 'What must be need not necessarily be!' Here is encouragement to shape our prayers and our planning quite differently.

Note, finally, how hesitantly the women approach the empty tomb (vv. 1–3): a model for us, approaching this holy shrine on Easter Day. Note how angels steer open minds towards unimagined possibilities (vv. 4–6), something that God's Spirit will still do today. Note the gospel clarity of the angelic announcement—'He is not here; he has risen!' (v. 6)—which challenges our tired Western faith. Note, too, the shameful cynicism that dismissed the truth as 'nonsense' (vv. 9–11), and Peter's mindless rush for evidence that remained for a while unsatisfied (v. 12). Yes, this is indeed a great and terrible day that casts faith and life in a brand new light. Here is our finally stopping point and the glorious climax of Holy Week. Happy Easter!

FURTHER READING

A.E. McGrath, *Luther's Theology of the Cross*, Blackwells, 1985.

A.M. Ramsey, *The Resurrection of Christ*, Collins, 1966.

J.R.W. Stott, *The Cross of Christ*, IVP, 1986.

H.A. Williams, *True Resurrection*, Mitchell Beazley, 1972.

THE RESURRECTION

The death and resurrection of Jesus are central to the Christian faith; these events that happened two thousand years ago continue to inform, transform and inspire millions of lives. In these next days we will reflect on both some of the post-Resurrection encounters (Mary in the garden, the Emmaus road disciples and Peter), and the doctrine of the resurrection as expressed by the apostles Paul and John.

These readings illustrate that Jesus Christ towers over history, yet also meets individuals in their daily lives and at their point of need. We need these two perspectives.

There is a short exercise to accompany each reading. The aim is to allow time to engage more deeply with God in his word and to grasp a little more firmly the good gifts he has given us in Jesus, so that we may more fully live his risen life.

Quotations are taken from the New International Version of the Bible.

24–30 MARCH

1 Mary, called by name

John 20:1–18

Mary has no awareness that her Lord is no longer dead: she is immersed in grief (v. 11). Note the kindness of the angels, who ask an obvious question but thereby meet Mary in her pain. One of the saddest statements of scripture is her assertion that the grave has been robbed, as she discovers that the body has gone (v. 13). Jesus repeats the angels' question as he comes into Mary's view. As in his earlier ministry, he meets her where she is, in her ignorance and despair. Then comes one of the most personal yet awesome moments in history: the God of creation bringing news of resurrection to a woman broken by grief (v. 16).

This is the pattern for each of us and for our broken world. In the midst of life with its sorrows, joys and mysteries, God calls each by name. In that instant, transformation began for Mary: her worldview changed, her despair turned to hope and her own life was given eternal significance as she absorbed the truth of Jesus risen from death.

By his Spirit today, Jesus lives in us and is with us. The imagination is part of our God-given humanity and can help us encounter God. In this exercise, imagine a place where you feel at ease—a garden or a wild landscape or a favourite known place. Take time to picture some details, such as colour and weather. Still in your imagination, settle yourself in one part of the picture. Become aware that Jesus is there with you. He asks what you are thinking about, and how you are. Respond honestly.

Then hear him simply speak your name, as he spoke Mary's; he speaks with kindness, knowing you and loving you. How do you want to respond? Look at him and say what is on your heart. It is important to him. For a few minutes, stay in his presence, receiving what he wants to bring you today. Like Mary, we can know healing and hope as we listen to the risen Jesus.

You may like to reflect on this imaginative encounter and thank God for his love for you.

2 A cosmic event

Colossians 1:15–23

Paul is writing this letter from prison in Rome to refute heretical teaching taking hold of the young church at Colossae. This human philosophy was empty and incapable of transforming lives; Christ, however, towers above history as creator (v. 16), sustainer (v. 17), head of the Church, the first to rise from death with a resurrection body (v. 18), God in human form (v. 19), and the one who reconciles (vv. 20–22). This is the cosmic Christ: words cannot do justice to the supreme place he has. This one calls out our worship—our 'yes' to his place in creation, in the Church and in our lives. Yet not only is he above all things but he has also stooped beneath all things to make peace 'through his blood, shed on the cross' (v. 20). His extraordinary sacrifice reveals the love of God to all who would respond.

Do you hear the strength of Paul's declaration, his confidence in the work of God on our behalf? 'But now he has reconciled you… to present you holy in his sight' (v. 22). Paul knew how easily Christians can be 'moved' (v. 23) from standing on the rock of Christ. He longed for the Colossians to know the peace and the privileges of the gospel, and to know with confidence the reality of sharing in the future resurrection (see 1:5). This is the big picture to hold on to, the worldview to grasp. It will help to keep our inevitable trials in perspective.

If you can, read the passage aloud, slowly, two or three times. Is there a phrase that catches your attention? Stay with that phrase (or phrases), and reflect on it. Chew it over. Receive into yourself its truth. The Holy Spirit may be highlighting something for you.

Turn your reflections into prayer: talk to God naturally; be yourself. Finally, receive God's peace, his gift, in a moment or two of silence. May the word of God dwell in you richly.

3 He walks alongside

Luke 24:13–35

This powerful account of one of Jesus' resurrection appearances has inspired artists down the centuries; it has a visual and emotional drama that engages us.

At first we wonder why the disciples don't recognize Jesus or why he chooses not to reveal his identity. They are immersed in disappointment. Jesus allows them time to articulate their dashed hope (v. 21). He not only brings them reassurance that he is indeed risen, thus rekindling their hope in him as Messiah; he also meets their need to understand things from God's perspective—that this Messiah would suffer before entering glory, and that these things are spoken of throughout scripture (vv. 25–27). Thus their deep spiritual hunger is fed.

Like these two disciples, aren't we often immersed in our own perspective, especially as we grapple with real anguish or disappointment? The Emmaus road story illustrates that God knows our need to understand; like them, we are sometimes left waiting as we walk on in life. Remember that Jesus is concerned for us to articulate our deep desires. The risen Christ walks alongside.

In an attitude of quiet and openness, become aware that the loving Lord is with you. You may like to rest your hands, palms upwards, on your knees, as a symbol of this openness. Is there a desire that awaits fulfilment? A dashed hope? A disappointment with God? Jesus wants to hear your story, your perspective. Tell him.

He has heard you. Quietly be receptive to the Spirit of God: he loves to reassure, to speak and to fill you with his Spirit. The risen Jesus will bring spiritual food to you, so receive it in faith, even if feelings are absent.

Thank God that he walks with you today. One day we will understand fully, even as we are fully understood, known and loved (1 Corinthians 13:12). We have a glorious hope that nothing can destroy.

'When I tried to understand… it was oppressive to me till I entered the sanctuary of God; then I understood' (Psalm 73:16).

4 The indescribable gift

1 Corinthians 15:17–28, 50–58

This week my son is revising for exams: he needs to remember the term's work. We humans easily forget, whether it's a name, a phone number or, more profoundly, key truths that dictate how we end up living our lives. 'Stand firm. Let nothing move you,' exhorts Paul (v. 58). The resurrection of Jesus is foundational to our lives, both in issues of mental and spiritual well-being and in the choices we make in the light of it. This whole chapter is a reminder of astonishing grace.

First, the resurrection clinches the forgiveness of sin (v. 17), and second, Christ's resurrection is the guarantee of the resurrection of all of God's redeemed people (vv. 23, 51). Death itself, the last enemy, will be destroyed (vv. 26, 54–57). We struggle to conceive of life in eternity, but Paul sums it up: 'Just as we have borne the likeness of the earthly man, so shall we bear the likeness of the man from heaven' (v. 49). All this is a given victory from God, on our behalf: 'He gives us the victory through our Lord Jesus Christ' (v. 57).

Paul reminds the Corinthians in 15:1 of what they have received. Rest your hands, cupped open on your lap, and receive as you remember:

- Remember with thanks Jesus' death on your behalf. 'It is finished' (John 19:30). Receive his forgiveness and his empowering to live, and 'give yourself fully to the work of the Lord' (v. 58), wherever that takes you at present.

- Remember with thanks that Jesus has triumphed over death for you: one day you will exchange the clothes of mortality for those of immortality. Receive this resurrection promise for yourself. God wants his people to be confident and to know freedom from fear. The best is yet to be! 'All shall be well, and all manner of things shall be well' (Julian of Norwich).

'Thanks be to God for his indescribable gift!' (2 Corinthians 9:15).

5 Life is for love

1 John 4:7–21

To be Christ's is to walk in love; God's love is now incarnate in us, made possible by Jesus' resurrection power given to all believers (v. 13). To be on the receiving end of Christian love—be it a timely phone call, a meal shared or a loving prayer in a crisis—is to receive the love of God. As we give these things, we experience something of the completeness (v. 17) that renders us more fully human, and we discover the joy that Jesus promised would accompany walking in the Spirit (John 15:11).

God, in his infinite wisdom, has made us all different, so how we express this life will vary. For centuries, prayerful people have discovered guidance for their day and for their life by identifying two contrasting responses. As they ask themselves the questions, 'For what am I most grateful?' and 'For what am I least grateful?' they can identify moments of 'consolation' and 'desolation'. Another way of putting this would be to ask, 'When did I give or receive most love today?' and 'When did I give or receive least?'

This exercise, done regularly, can help us tune in to how God has made us. It is not a selfish occupation, but rather a cooperation with him, so that we might be more truly who he has made us and free to express Christ in ways that are appropriate. We gradually find that we sense what we should do more of and what to do less. For example, I experience a personal call to be a 'nurturer', in that I sense joy when I am nurturing, be it children, adults, plants, family or friends.

God is love (v. 16): sit before him, grateful for his care for you today, and relax. Ask for the Spirit's help as you gently reflect on the day (or previous day). What do you feel grateful for? When did you feel fully alive… more complete? The answer could be a small thing: just let the day play back and savour again the good moments (consolation).

Still relaxed, play back the times that drained life from you or were hard (desolation). Just notice them and try not to judge.

Offer these reflections to God. Is he saying anything to you through them? Thank him for his love, and trust that he will give you opportunities to give and receive the life and love that flow from the resurrection of Jesus.

6 Known, healed and sent

John 21:1–19

Peter was a natural leader: we see that here as he heads up the job of dragging the nets ashore (v. 11). What formed him for ministry, though, and for fulfilling God's greater purposes, was the inner surrender of his sinful, weak character (exposed for us all to see in the threefold denial, John 18:15–27) to the risen Jesus. In this encounter, the Lord knows that the charcoal fire will evoke the shame and despair of that dark night.

Jesus prepares the way by meeting Peter's frustrations in fishing: he extravagantly provides a huge catch (vv. 6, 11). The Lord demonstrates his love, as the catch is followed by the kind provision of a cooked breakfast.

As the disciples take in the impact and implications of seeing their risen Lord, Jesus completes the healing in Peter, calling out from him three declarations of love, countering the three denials. Peter now speaks as one who has experienced acceptance and forgiveness, no longer depending on his own meagre resources. This is a great shift, and each of us must make this painful yet liberating journey if we are truly to glorify God (v. 19). 'We love because he first loved us' (1 John 4:19).

The challenge for us is to allow Jesus to expose those unhealed or unredeemed parts of us. We may, like Peter, have natural gifts, but they can be marred or useless if our inner life (or 'heart' as the Bible calls it) is not touched by his grace. Our culture of 'living on the outside' mitigates against this, but what a blessing it is when we, like Peter, have surrendered our entire personality, all that drives us. It's a kind of death

(Romans 6:4), but only in order that Christ's resurrection may be manifest in us. What a glorious thing!

Peter went on to an extraordinary but costly life of faith, teaching, leading and pastoring. This far outstripped the life he had lived in his own strength. The key question to Peter from Jesus was not about how much he might achieve or how good a fisherman he was. It was about love: 'Do you love me?' Love gives itself. Jesus releases Peter to give himself to the one who gave himself for him. Out of this flows his future.

- What are one or two of your natural strengths? What do you like to do? Thank God for these gifts.
- Are you aware of any inner need for Jesus' healing? Take a moment to name this need and then to offer it to him, your Redeemer.
- Like Peter, offer your whole being to Jesus, so that his resurrection may fill your day-by-day life and ministries.

Guidelines

This week we have taken time to allow familiar truths and events to touch, inform and inspire us. We have seen the ways Jesus approached, met and spoke with some of his followers after his resurrection, and how two of those followers wrote out of their reflections on that great event. We have seen how grief, disappointment and moral failure are addressed by the risen Lord.

In our flawed humanity, we can despair, and fear that the help we are offered is 'too good to be true'. The resurrection gifts of forgiveness, a glorious life begun in the now but continuing beyond death, and the ongoing presence of the risen Jesus, renewing us constantly, are generous indeed. Yet these gifts are real and true, and reasons for deep joy and grateful lives.

On this subject of gratitude, in Luke 17:11–19 we read of ten lepers healed by Jesus. 'One of them, when he saw he was healed, came back, praising God in a loud voice. He threw himself at Jesus' feet and thanked him' (vv. 15–16). Don't you love that energy—the loud voice and the throwing of himself before Jesus? The healed Samaritan puts the praise where it is due—to the loving Lord, whose compassion has delivered him from social exclusion and physical torment. This is a response that brings delight to God's heart; it gives God his rightful, glorious place, but also frees the recipient to live with an open heart. Living gratefully keeps us in a healthy dependence on God as we daily acknowledge his grace in our lives.

Take a few moments to sit before the Lord with open hands. Pour out a litany of gratitude to him, both for the small mercies and for the great gifts we have looked at this week. Allow him to energize you afresh as you remain open to more of his grace and resurrection power for you. Ask to be filled with his Spirit and thank him; let that joy be released in and through you, to God's glory. Christ is risen! He is risen indeed!

'Give thanks to the Lord, for he is good. His love endures forever' (Psalm 136:1).

JOB

In this masterpiece of poetry, the traditional Israelite solution to the problem of suffering is radically reviewed. Job's innocent suffering calls into question the whole system of rewards and punishments in this life, despite the vain efforts of his friends to shore it up by urging him to admit his guilt, or at least his pride, or even that he must have sinned unwittingly. The uncertainties, frustrations, mood swings and anger of the sufferer are presented with fearless vigour. Job does not hesitate to rail against his tormentor and to accuse God of bullying and rank injustice. At the same time, in protesting his innocence (which the reader knows from the Prologue) and rejecting the shallow solutions of the sages, Job clings blindly to God. Even when shrinking from God's torments, Job is confident of God's unfailing care. Paradoxically, although he sees no possibility of a future life, he is somehow sure that after his death he will know God's vindication. In the end, his trust is justified by an overwhelming experience of the majesty, power and wisdom of God. The reader is left, however, with the feeling that the author did not intend to produce a simple solution to the problem of suffering.

The discourses are best understood as being written soon after the exile to Babylon, as a reflection on and questioning of the sufferings then being undergone. Dramatically, however, they are set in an earlier nomadic period before the revelation of the Lord. Job is the name of one of three traditional wise men mentioned in Ezekiel 14:14. The setting of the dialogue in Uz, far to the east, locates it in the land of sages and allows free discussion of the problem of suffering without explicit reference to Israelite revelation, until the appearance of the Lord in chapter 38. The clear structure of the four-cornered dispute is interrupted by two elements: by the hymn in praise of Wisdom (ch. 28), which differs in its view of Wisdom from that held by either Job or his friends, and by the speeches of Elihu (chs. 32—37), which merely repeat the problem already stated and pre-empt the solution still to come. Both these elements may well stem from the main author of the book, but are not clearly integrated into the dialogue.

As in other ancient Near Eastern Wisdom writings, the poetic dispute is set within a prose framework. Paradoxically, the final twofold restoration of Job's wealth gives a different and more comforting solution to the problem of suffering than that offered by the poetic kernel of the book. Nor does the patient Job of the prose framework wholly accord with the intolerant and questioning rebel of the dialogues.

1 The heavenly court

Job 1

This most poetic of all the books of the Bible begins with a prose introduction to set the scene. The setting is the heavenly court, where God is surrounded by his courtiers—the 'sons of God', or the angels (v. 6). It is probably the most explicit of all the representations of heaven, the place where God resides, until the court scenes of the final book of the Bible, Revelation 4—5. In its turn it is inspired by Babylonian ideas of the heavenly court. Since God is the greatest of all monarchs, he must be surrounded by the greatest of all courts. More detail crops up elsewhere (notably in Ezekiel 1), and we learn that there are cherubim, who are modelled on the great Babylonian stone carvings of the guardians of the temples—awesome creatures with wings (for total mobility), a headful of horns (for strength and aggressive power), and plenty of eyes (for penetrating vision). There are also seraphim, whose name means 'burning ones', and who are represented as fiery serpents. Further details about these heavenly creatures abound in the later legends and in the Jewish literature after the end of the Old Testament. They are all there to carry out the bidding of the Lord: they are powers of God, extending the divine will to the ends of the universe.

Among them is Satan. He is not yet seen as a fallen angel: this development comes only later. He is the angel who is charged with testing out people on earth; indeed, this is what the name 'Satan' means —'the tester'. As yet, he is a loyal servant of the Lord, although we must admit that in the little dialogue we are given here, he is a pretty cheeky one! 'You get on with your business,' he implies, 'and I'll get on with mine.' He is quite happy to answer back to the Almighty, telling him that he is too starry-eyed, and that Job is loyal only because and only as long as he is well blessed with the good things of life.

The notion that God directly imposes temptation is slightly worrying and, indeed, one of the functions of Satan in the story is to avoid too direct a link between God and temptation. God is, of course, ultimately responsible for everything that goes on, and Job's loyalty (like that of any of us) must be tested out. But God cannot directly entice Job into betrayal; that is Satan's job.

2 The testing complete

Job 2

Job has survived the first test, which occasions a second scene where Satan is even cheekier than in the first. With that love of repetition which is so typical of the oral storyteller, Job answers back with the same 'You get on with your business...' and then adds more. We are reminded of that delicious scene in Genesis 18, where Abraham shows the same impertinence (a little more apologetically) in bargaining with God for the sparing of Sodom from its fate.

What 'Skin for skin!' (or 'Skin after skin', NJB) means is difficult to fathom exactly. It is obviously some proverb, but neither 'an eye for an eye' nor 'six of one and half-a-dozen of the other' fits the bill. Perhaps 'you scratch my back and I'll scratch yours' fits the context best: if God smiles on Job, Job will smile back at God. But why 'skin for skin' rather than some such formula as 'gift for gift', or 'one good deed deserves another'?

Anyway, the ensuing disasters have tripped one on another's heels with dramatic thoroughness, leaving Job with neither possessions nor family—only his wife, to whom, as we will later learn (19:17), his breath smells. It is one thing to be deprived of the good things of life, the super-fluities that enhance one's enjoyment, but the loss of beloved family and crippling sickness touch the very being. In both these cases, we must cry out at the injustice, 'What has the innocent done?' or 'Why me?' The first harsh lesson of the book of Job is that there is no question of justice when you are dealing with God. God does not work in this way—just as, in the parable of the workers in the vineyard (Matthew 20:1–16), we can't complain at God's generosity to the undeserving who get the same reward as those who have deserved it.

The thought of a heavenly reward in the afterlife is not the answer to Job's problem. This possibility had not yet surfaced in the beliefs of the time, nor is it satisfying. This cannot be the full meaning of Luke's version of the Beatitudes: 'Blessed are you who are poor… who are hungry [yes, the actual poor, the actual hungry], for you will be filled' (6:20–21, NRSV). There must be something significant about the sufferer's love of God, and ultimate trust and confidence in God, being tempered and tried in the furnace and coming out purified and strengthened, all the alloys of comfort and human ties having been purged away. It is not easy to understand or to accept.

3 Job's curse

Job 3

Once Job's proverbial comforters have taken up position and sat on the ground beside him for seven days and seven nights, Job begins the poetic part of the book by launching straight into a comprehensive curse of the day he was born and the night he was conceived. He shows the depths of his distress and the total absence of any hope—or *almost* total absence. He never even contemplates suicide, which may already suggest the thinnest of threads of hope, or perhaps simply of obedience and acceptance of the testing imposed on him. Indeed, it is a sign of the deep faith which is the background of all the biblical writings that there is only one instance of suicide in the whole of the Hebrew Bible: Ahitophel, the counsellor of David, who betrayed his master and went over to David's rebellious son, Absalom. When Absalom rejects Ahitophel's advice and Ahitophel realizes that David will triumph, he goes off and hangs himself (2 Samuel 17:23). Ahitophel's mode of suicide is, of course, the model in Matthew 27:5 for that of Judas, who also betrayed his master.

Job's longing for peace, 'Now I should be lying in peace, wrapped in a restful slumber, with the kings and high viziers of earth' (vv. 13–14, NJB), is slightly less ashen than many of the descriptions of Sheol, the place of the dead. The hope of resurrection was not yet part of the

Hebrew picture. The earliest conception of death was of being gathered to the ancestors—typical of early tribal culture. We do not know what this involved on the level of personal consciousness. The most we can find is David's sorrowful comment when his infant son dies: 'I shall go to him but he cannot come back to me' (2 Samuel 12:23). Later comes the notion of Sheol, a sort of underworld for the dead.

Job pictures himself cocooned in restful slumber, but the horror of Sheol was in the powerlessness it bestowed. The dead there have no strength. They cannot even praise God: 'Can shadows rise up to praise you?' says the psalmist (Psalm 88:10, NJB). When the great king of Babylon arrives in Sheol, the dead have power only to rise and mock him bitterly—'So, you too are now as weak as we are'—before sinking down again (I imagine like dead leaves at the bottom of a pond), 'under you a mattress of maggots, over you a blanket of worms' (Isaiah 14:9–11).

4 Eliphaz suggests a solution

Job 4

It makes me boil with rage even to listen to the slimy self-righteousness of Eliphaz. What must it have done to Job? Eliphaz is so sure of himself, so confident of his own analysis of his experience, and at the same time starts with such oily courtesy. To add to that, he then produces an eerie and insubstantial revelation that he received in a dream-situation (vv. 12–14), with a sort of apology that in such a situation you are too sleepy and confused to be sure of anything. He doesn't tell Job what the revelation was, which makes it all the more powerful. You can't contradict something you have not been plainly told, but it gets under your skin all the same—even more so, perhaps. Then Eliphaz has the effrontery to guess the obvious: if God cannot rely even on his own servants, the angels (v. 18), Job *must* have committed some fault and needs only to admit it.

It is all part of the drama that the reader should be driven to fury— and poor Job too, on his ash heap, agonizingly scratching his ulcers with his piece of broken pottery (2:7). The three wise men from the east, which was always the fountainhead of wisdom (even before the Beatles discovered it), are sent specifically to give the answers suggested by the prosaic wisdom of Israel at the time, specifically to show the barrenness of popular philosophy. For Job on his ash heap, substitute the exiled Israelite in Babylon, whose father was dragged over the desert on a meat-hook (for so the Babylonians claimed). What had the second-generation exile done to deserve his suffering? He could no more sing a song to the Lord in Babylon than could the powerless denizens of Sheol: 'How could we sing a song of Yahweh on alien soil?' (Psalm 137:4).

It is appropriate, for the purposes of the drama and the posing of the question that dominates the book—the agonized cry of injustice raised against the God of all justice—that every element of the revelation of God should be muted and withdrawn. Once the dramatic prose intro-duction is over and we are launched into the poetic dialogues, we are in a Godless world, blind to any revelation from the Lord—until his final explosive appearance. That is why the platitudes of wisdom, no doubt offered also to the unsatisfied second generation of exiles in Babylon, can be presented in all their banality.

5 The tireless watcher

Job 7

Never, to my knowledge, have the agonies of sickness been so hauntingly evoked as in this passage. Job's reflections are full of contradictions or mood swings: the long nights of tossing and turning and waiting for day, swinging to the days that pass like a weaver's shuttle (chucked from one side of the weighted threads to the other); the longing for sleep, which is then tortured by nightmares and apparitions. Most of all, there is the mood swing with regard to God's constant surveillance. Job is thoroughly dependent on that surveillance, dreading that God might take his sus-taining eye off him for a moment so that he will cease to be ('the eye that once saw me will look on me no more; your eyes will turn my way, and I shall not be there', v. 8), and yet the impatience to be left alone in peace ('Am I the Sea, or some sea monster, that you should keep me under guard? ... Will you never take your eyes off me long enough for me to swallow my spittle?', vv. 12, 19). Job twists this way and that, longing to be free but clinging to his divine tormentor. He admits his guilt ('Can you not tolerate my sin?', v. 21a) but obviously does not feel that this is damaging to his cause. He even, finally, almost taunts God, supposing that God comes too late to look for him ('you will look for me and I shall be no more', v. 21b).

This agony is like the agonies of conscience—the knowledge that there is, unseen and immovable in the shadows, a firm pillar or rock, an unchanging standard that cannot be tricked, on which one relies, despite all failure to adhere to it. In the drama, of course, Job has no knowledge of God or of the revelation to Israel of a loving God—certainly not of the Lord revealed to Moses after the first betrayal of the covenant, a God of 'tenderness and compassion, slow to anger, rich in faithful love and constancy' who forgives faults to thousands (Exodus 34:6–7). This is why the drama is set in the mythical land of Oz, in the ancient nomadic world of wandering sages. The author deliberately leaves this revelation and its accompanying worldview out of consideration, being dissatisfied with the simple solutions it offers. They provide no satisfying answer to the undeserved suffering that he is struggling to understand. That is why Job can admit sin and find in this admission no solution.

6 The laughter of the all-powerful unjust Judge

Job 9

There is no arguing with this God. He does what he will and none can gainsay him; he acts like a petulant and irresponsible child whom no one can call to book. He does not even deign to answer an accusation, but laughs at the plight of the innocent. Job even tries to pretend to laugh with him, though filled with fear at the knowledge that God persists in looking on him as guilty. Perhaps (such is the depths of his confusion) he actually is guilty: 'But am I innocent? I am no longer sure' (v. 21).

You can't get to grips with this God who defies the laws of nature. This God is not answerable to anybody. There are no standards to which this God must adhere. There is no chance of comfortably representing this God as an old man sitting on a cloud, no reassurance of creating God in our own image. It is the splendour and greatness of the book of Job to give a glimpse of the unknowable, the awesome, the daunting. The God of the philosophers whom we encounter here is not like anything, does not fit into any categories, that we can conceive. Everything said about this God must be contradicted. This God creates—and destroys. This God lays down mountains—only to remove them. This God sets a sun in the heavens—only to forbid it to rise. This God institutes justice—only to laugh at its rules. It is an Alice-in-Wonderland world where things happen unpredictably, as unpredictable as the adults' world seems to children, for it is not built on child's logic.

No more is God answerable to our logic. God loves, but not in the way that we love. God knows, but 'my thoughts are not your thoughts' (Isaiah 55:8). The first step towards God is to give in and admit that all is beyond our comprehension, for we cannot demand a rationale from God. This is where the graciousness and gentleness of revelation comes in: we are lost and totally disorientated, at which God comforts us in this incomprehensible world by showing us, at least, that he cares for us. But Job, not satisfied with the platitudes of his so-called 'friends', which are based on that revelation, discards all this comfort and is left in the great cloud of unknowing. It takes courage to look truth in the face and to ask the questions beyond our familiar comfort zone.

Guidelines

There is Job, on his ash heap, comfortless. He is as comfortless as the millions of people, over the ages and today, in a godless world, who do not have the solidity of faith to rely on. We all, at one time or another, share this faithlessness ('Lord, I believe. Help my unbelief!') and can appreciate both the desolate loneliness of that world and the reassurance of the care of a loving God revealed to us first in the Hebrew tradition, and then, fully and finally, in Jesus Christ, the incarnate image of the Father.

Lord, I thank you for the gift of this faith, for the ability to know you through your Son, Jesus Christ. I ask you to keep me steadfast in this faith, ever to appreciate your gift and to intensify its meaning and out-working in my life. I know my frailty, my wobbles, my unpredictability, my neglect of your quiet care, of your loving respect for my free choice to turn my back on you. Draw me always back to you, to meditate on you and to appreciate more and more my need for you and the way you satisfy that need in my life.

1 Hope against hope

Job 14

Job seems to be at the depths of despair, the end of his tether. Another of his 'friends', Zophar, has ladled out some platitudes to him (ch. 11), eloquently insisting that God knows everything and that Job must have sinned. All Job needs to do is acknowledge his sin and beg forgiveness, then he will sleep secure and no one will trouble him; to which Job replies with bitter sarcasm, 'Doubtless… when you die, wisdom will die with you' (12:2). Life just isn't like that, he says, for 'the tents of brigands are left in peace: those who provoke God dwell secure' (12:6). Job never doubts God's wisdom, but it is paradoxical, for God arranges everything at will, drought as well as flood. God also turns things upside down at will, turning judges into fools, stripping off the regalia of kings, robbing seniors of their wits (12:13–15). Then Job formally and legally challenges God to bring his evidence: 'Tell me what my misdeed has been, what my sin' (13:23).

Job now lapses into sarcasm against God: how can you fix your gaze on a human being, 'fleeting as a shadow, transient' (14:2)? A human being is worse off than a felled tree, for a felled tree, 'let it scent the water, and it buds', but 'a human being, once laid to rest, will never rise again' (v. 12). And yet, after this firm statement of the finality of human death, Job utters his first wisp of hope, with the suggestion that, if he is hidden away in Sheol for long enough, God might fix a day for calling him to mind: 'you would seal up my crime in a bag, and put a cover over my fault' (v. 17).

The first trickle is beginning which would eventually issue in the full hope of eternal life. Job does not dare assert, but he questions, 'Can the dead come back to life?' (v. 14). The human spirit cannot accept that death is the ultimate end. Even the wretched, powerless half-life of Sheol is continued existence, and while there is existence (it can hardly be called 'life') there is hope. Even those who, in ancient religions, made offerings for the dead, or built sumptuous tombs at the roadside for passing travellers to admire, must have thought that some sort of existence continued which would be enriched by such attentions. There burns a glimmer of hope even in Job's hopelessness.

2 Cover not my blood, O earth!

Job 16

Rapidly Eliphaz sets about extinguishing the glimmer of hope: he rails against Job's effrontery and lack of reverence in daring to confront God and question the divine decisions. No good can come to one who defies Shaddai (15:25). The divine name 'El Shaddai', which comes occasionally in the dialogue of Job, has never been satisfactorily explained. It is a very ancient name for God, possibly brought by Abraham from Mesopotamia (Genesis 17:1). The meaning 'God of the mountains' is a possibility, or 'God of the open deserts', depending on the Mesopotamian word from which it is derived. When the Bible came to be translated into Greek, the translators inserted into it their own theology, rendering it by the awesome *Pantocrator* or 'All-powerful', now so reminiscent of those great mosaic icons in the apses of Byzantine churches. Whatever the name means, however, its function in Job is to indicate that we are outside the sphere of the privileged Hebrew-Israelite revelation.

Job's reply to Eliphaz is again impatience at these platitudes. Then he turns to rail furiously against the pitiless injustice of God. Once again he vigorously protests his innocence. In the face of God's constant attack ('He shoots his arrows at me from all sides... Breach after breach he drives through me', vv. 13, 14) Job calls on the earth not to cover his blood, for blood cries out for vengeance. So he will have a dual witness crying for vengeance: on earth his uncovered blood, in heaven his constant crying. This prolonged cry of Job is perhaps the most desperate of all: there is no light, no relief. He sees no hope—but he still does not contemplate suicide. He still believes in God and believes that somehow his crying will not go unheeded. He may rail against God's injustice but he still believes that somehow he will get justice, or he would not cry out!

This is some comfort when we ourselves are desperate in our own troubles and see no hope and no solution. If we believe in God—even a neglectful God—we can still cry for help. Job, in his desperate situation, when he can see no vestige of hope or promise, still cries out. As an agnostic friend of mine once said, 'If you are lost in the fog, you still cry "Help!" even if you don't know that there is anybody to hear you.'

3 I know that my Redeemer liveth

Job 19

In chapter 18 it was Bildad of Shuah's turn to tell Job that the wicked come to a bad end. 'Stuff and nonsense,' says Job again, 'I know that God has wronged me'. Then he launches into a detailed description of God's bullying—how God, with superior strength, blocks every path and treats Job as an enemy. A new and pathetic element is the mockery by Job's servants, who pretend not to know him (v. 15), and mockery by children, who jeer at him as soon as he stands up (v. 18). Those he loved best have turned against him and even his wife cannot bear his stench. Then at last he breaks down before his cruel 'comforters': 'Pity me, pity me, my friends' (v. 21).

However, this abandonment seems to give him comfort and renew his strength, for within two verses he pronounces the greatest of all paeans of hope. So sure is his hope that he would have it engraved on rock as an eternal memorial. Job still seems to envisage that he is near death, but this hope will survive him, and there will be an awakening at which God will receive him.

The 'Defender' or 'Redeemer' is, in Hebrew, *go'el*, a wonderful concept of Jewish family unity (Numbers 35:19). The *go'el* is the nearest male relative, who stands by the person in distress as a last resort, and will never desert the unfortunate family member. If I am forced to the ultimate disaster of selling my ancestral land, my last means of support, my *go'el* is bound to buy it back for me. If I marry and die childless, my *go'el* is bound to marry my wife and bring up an heir to my name (not his own name). Here the *go'el* will take his stand (a technical legal term) as Job's defender in court.

The passage is full of difficulties. Is the Redeemer God himself? Certainly 'I shall look on God... my eyes will be gazing on no stranger' (vv. 26–27), but it may be that this is only after the Defender has done his job. What does 'from my flesh' mean (v. 26)? It could imply a vigorous affirmation of bodily resurrection, but equally well it could mean 'out of my flesh' in the sense of 'freed from my flesh'. And 'rise up last' (v. 25) could equally well mean 'at the last', as though some final scene was envisaged. Whatever the details, it is a staunch and inspiring expression of hope.

4 A hymn to Wisdom

Job 28

If there were any low points in the book of Job, one could speak of this hymn as one of the high points. This splendid poem to divine Wisdom concludes the conversations between Job and his 'comforters', and serves as an introduction to the final part of the book and its divine revelation. The book of Job is about the search for wisdom and understanding— understanding of the mystery of evil, of undeserved suffering—and after the problem has been fully posed, before the resolution, comes this hymn to divine Wisdom. The Wisdom literature of the Old Testament (of which Job is a part) is firmly based on the idea that all wisdom comes from God and is, indeed, a manifestation of God. This is the chief mark that distinguishes this group of writings from other Wisdom writings of the ancient world, that true wisdom cannot be reached by unaided human effort but can only be granted by the Lord. It is an attractive idea that this poem is based on an ancient myth about the search for wisdom, which finally only God can find.

The poem is divided into three sections, the first two concluding with the refrain, 'But where does Wisdom come from? Where is Intelligence to be found?' (vv. 12, 20). The first section celebrates human ingenuity and discovery, particularly exploration of the earth's resources. The second section, by contrast, declares that true Wisdom, to which all earthly treasures are as nothing, is nowhere to be found. The final section turns to God, the only source of true Wisdom, 'that is fear of the Lord'.

For Christians, Christ is the Wisdom of God, the fulfilment of the wisdom for which the Bible is searching. The apostle Paul calls Christ 'the power... and the wisdom of God' (1 Corinthians 1:24), and the prologue of the Gospel of John hymns the Word of God, who was with God in the beginning before the world was, and is the principle or template of creation—the image in God according to which God creates, and in which creation reaches its fullness. The Wisdom literature is building towards this completion when it personifies Wisdom as 'a reflection of the eternal light, untarnished mirror of God's active power' (Wisdom of Solomon 7:26). Another lovely poem, Ben Sira 24, celebrates Wisdom as the Law which has 'taken root in a privileged people', and 'grown tall as a palm in En-Gedi' (vv. 12, 14). In Christ, all Wisdom is to be found, the completion of the revelation of the Lord.

5 Contrasts

Job 29

Disregarding all the presumably well-meaning advice he has received from his companions, Job finishes his speech with this heartrending summing-up, contrasting his former dignity with his present misery. The major emphasis of the contrast is new, although it has surfaced occasionally. Most of Job's complaints have been about the physical discomfort, the lack of companionship, or—worse—the mental and spiritual anguish of God's bullying oppression, and the consequent hopelessness of finding any justice or vindication of the innocence on which he insists. Now he turns to the social respect and civic dignity that he once had and has now lost.

The contrast is, as always, brilliantly painted. The society that the author shows us is one in which respect for age and wisdom is paramount. In such a society, there was presumably no appointed magistracy, no democratically elected assembly, still less a hereditary monarchy. Respect had to be won by personal qualities. Decisions were made by the elders gathered at the gate (as, in other societies, on the village green or in the pub), and Job's wisdom above all was honoured, as 'young men stepped aside and... old men rose to their feet' (v. 8). The men of note, who broke off their speeches and put their hands over their mouths (v. 9), were presumably ashamed of what they had just said by comparison to the wisdom pronounced by Job. Not only was he honoured in public life but he was blessed for his attention to the poor and needy, an attention that does not always accompany a reputation for wisdom. In Hebrew society and Hebrew Wisdom literature, however, wisdom is always a practical and active gift.

The point of view is definitely aristocratic, and Job rather lets himself down when, in chapter 30, he comes to describe the people who now tease, mock and torment him. All sympathy for the poor and destitute seems to have deserted him as he contemptuously describes those who 'make their meals off roots of broom' and 'huddle together in the thistles' (30:4, 7). We are tempted to say that, all along, his sin may well have been arrogance, and that if he treated these people like that and thought of them with such contempt in the day of his well-being, he now deserves all he gets! Perhaps, though, allowance should be made for a little literary flourish on the part of the author.

6 Job's final defence

Job 31

In his final defence, Job makes a series of conditional curses on himself if he has committed each particular sort of failing. This was a resort in Israelite law: in certain cases where evidence was lacking, the official responsible could pronounce a curse on a suspect, to which the suspect must reply 'Amen' in provisional acceptance of the curse if guilty. This was sufficient to establish innocence. However, there is no other such extended proclamation of innocence as this in the Bible. An interesting parallel in Egyptian Wisdom literature occurs in the Egyptian *Book of the Dead*, where the dead person is required to give a similar recital of innocence before entering the Egyptian equivalent of eternal rest.

Job's recital is impressively comprehensive, covering not only a careful list of sins of commission, but also a wide-ranging list of sins of omission. It starts with sexual sins, wonderfully reminiscent of the teaching of Jesus: lust of the eyes is already a sin. There follows deceit, perhaps especially in business dealings (vv. 5–8). Next comes the more delicate sin which would, today, be called harassment of the weak and defence-less (vv. 13–15), a reminder that in Israel even slaves had rights, and that the protection of the law was intended to leave every person standing tall and confident before the Lord. Soon come the sins of omission, as Job considers the groups of the needy to whom the well-to-do must be sensitive (vv. 16–23). Then comes the more interior attitude of putting trust in gold (vv. 24–25), the self-satisfaction of achievement—echoed by the haunting parable of the rich fool, who built himself larger barns to store his crops, only to die that same night (Luke 12:16–21). There follows the superstition of false gods, blowing a kiss at the sun or the moon (vv. 26–27). The author may have been thinking of that dreadful scene of idolatry in the very courts of the temple on the eve of the Babylonian exile, which saw worshippers turned towards the rising sun with their backs to the sanctuary (Ezekiel 8:16). Some more subtle temptations of the rich and powerful follow: gloating over the less fortunate (v. 29), covering up one's failures, especially dishonesty (v. 33), diverting from the true course out of human respect for gossip or even family pressure (v. 34).

If Job—or anyone else, conscientiously examining their conduct—can claim innocence from all these faults, let them parade the writ of the accuser and flaunt it on their foreheads!

Guidelines

This week of readings has set out in all its strength the enigma of undeserved suffering. How can a just God permit it? Is there any fairness in God?

It has been called 'the problem of evil', but it is not exactly the problem of evil. The problem of evil—how God can permit evil in the world—is more a matter of free will. If God gives us the chance to love him, then we are given also the chance not to do so. And, if there is a genuine choice, at some times people will choose not to do so. It could, of course, also be called 'the problem of goodness'. We are not attracted to evil but to the manifold good things presented to us, and we sometimes choose one good thing when we should choose another good thing, which various circumstances make a better thing to choose. We are misled by God's very generosity.

The problem of undeserved suffering is different—a tsunami, a lightning strike, a child dying of leukaemia. Granted that the sins of the parents should not be visited on the children, this was the problem that faced the second generation of Jews in Babylon: their parents may have been unfaithful to the covenant but what of themselves? The book of Job is the reaction to that puzzle.

Lord, grant me patience and understanding. Grant me the trust to bear what suffering you send me. Grant me, above all, not to be judgmental, never to blame others for the sufferings they undergo.

1 Elihu appears

Job 32

Elihu is a puzzle. He appears suddenly, without any warning in the previous text. Of course, this is dramatically smoothed over in his introductory remarks, which represent him as staying silent and listening carefully throughout the previous discussions. He delicately excuses, or accounts for, his earlier silence on grounds of age and shyness: in his youth he has kept silent so that age could have its say, as is proper in the circumstances depicted in the book. But there are other problems: the names of all the other persons depicted fit the context of a drama in the ancient East, the land of Uz, the land of sages (whence come also the magi of the Gospel story). Elihu alone has a typical Hebrew name, compounded with 'God', like 'Israel' or 'Elijah' (= 'my God is Jahweh') or 'Elnathan' (= 'God gave'). Elihu means 'he is my God'. His clan is nicely chosen, for in Genesis 22:21 the two sons of Nahor (Abraham's brother, who stayed behind in the east when Abraham started his wanderings) are Uz (or Oz) and Buz. Uz is the homeland of the other sages, so Elihu is from the same stable of legendary wise men.

Nor do Elihu's words contribute much to the discussion. To a considerable extent, they repeat what has already been said or anticipate what is still to come. They certainly overlap with the solution to the problem of Job given by the Lord's appearing. Only Elihu's solution is rather more orthodox and less shocking. It is surprising that, speaking immediately afterwards, the Lord makes no allusion to Elihu's speeches in sentiments that overlap with his own! It is, finally, possible that the speeches of Elihu were added later precisely for this reason, to offer a more orthodox solution.

The literary style and approach are very similar to the earlier speeches, with plenty of description of the speaker's own feelings, which lie behind his words ('I have been waiting', v. 16) and rich, well-chosen imagery. Any writer or debater knows the feeling 'like new wine seeking a vent' (v. 19), which builds up until the words can no longer be held back and simply burst forth. However, there are also differences in the language, and the presence of Aramaic expressions and turns of phrase (which become increasingly common in Hebrew after the exile) suggest a later date.

Something has to be omitted to fit this splendid book into three weeks of readings, and I am sorry that the axe falls on Elihu!

2 The Lord replies

Job 38:1–35

We have heard the bitter, and not unjustified, complaints of Job against God. We have heard the feeble efforts of his companions to justify the divine ways. We have savoured the poem on divine Wisdom, which served as an interlude to finish the discussion. We have listened to Job's comprehensive self-defence. We have (perhaps) followed Elihu's speeches on God's behalf. And now, at last, we come to the towering response from the Lord in person. The build-up and the tension are quite deliberate, for the Lord is no ordinary person and the speeches are not to be tossed aside. Indeed, it is partly through their weight and their extent that they prevail.

No human being can see God and live. Moses had asked to see God's glory but the Lord put him in a cleft of the rock and shielded him until the glory had passed: 'you will see my back; but my face will not be seen' (Exodus 33:23). Elijah covered his face with his cloak before venturing out of the cave to experience God (1 Kings 19:13). Isaiah shrank from the cloud of God's glory in the temple, and even the fiery seraphim covered their faces (Isaiah 6:2) before the daunting sanctity of the Lord. The only response to the coming of the Lord is to hide in the rock: 'Go into the rock, hide in the dust, in terror of Yahweh, at the brilliance of his majesty, when he arises to make the earth quake' (Isaiah 2:10). The speeches given here in Job are an attempt to convey in words and poetry this experience of awe at the divine, and humility at the inadequacy of human nature. No logical answer is given to Job's complaints, but the experience of the divine is such that, by the end of these towering, cumulative speeches, no answer is necessary.

In this first response, the Lord replies in a tone of light sarcasm. It is not heavy and wounding sarcasm, but enough to mark the superiority of the Lord to any human accountability. Any woundingness of the sarcasm is muted by a certain playfulness. The dazzling recital of the wonders of nature that no human being can comprehend or explain forestalls any further questioning. There is no contempt, for the recital is permeated with a loving appreciation of the beauty of the creation, which has been rolled out for the joy and appreciation of the human inhabitants of this marvellous world.

3 The wonders of the animal kingdom

Job 38:36—39:35

Having interrogated Job about the seas, the earth, the weather and the stars, all of which are beyond human control or understanding, the Lord now proceeds to ask him whether he can account for the animals. The progress of science has made some of the lore invoked mysterious to us now.

The creature translated in 38:36 as 'ibis', in Hebrew, is *tuhot*, which seems to be the equivalent of Thoth, the Egyptian god of wisdom, who is represented as an ibis bird. The ibis, which appeared at a special season of the year, was reputed to foretell the flooding of the Nile; it certainly likes strutting around and fishing in shallow waters like those of the Nile flood. The cock's intelligence is easier to explain: he predicts the dawn just before it happens and, according to some lore, heralds the rain as well.

Next comes a series of animals who are famously self-reliant and far beyond human care. You don't need to feed a nursing lioness or a raven; they will find food anywhere! (38:39, 41). The birth processes of the mountain goats that roam the valleys round the Jordan must have seemed particularly unpredictable; these ibex are hard enough even to see as they meld into the sandy-coloured rock (39:1). The independent wild donkey (v. 5) is especially fascinating: he can still be glimpsed wandering the Judean desert and cropping something where there is palpably no greenery to eat. (I asked a bedhuin camel-boy once, 'What does he eat?' 'The ground,' he answered—and I supposed his English was limited.)

Woe betide you if you try to train a wild ox (or 'buffalo', v. 9)! They move in herds, and a single buffalo separated from the herd is notoriously fierce, equipped with a vicious pair of horns. The Greek translation here gives 'rhinoceros', and you can't push him around. The ostrich looks utterly stupid with her long bare neck and surprised expression but, stretching her long legs, she is faster than any horse and can break your arm with one blow of her head (v. 13). The war horse (v. 19), the biggest of all domestic animals (and especially big when compared with delicate little donkeys or mules), is also perhaps the most powerful, as crowds confronted with police horses well know.

The list ends, as it began, with two birds renowned for wisdom (v. 26). The hawk's reputation for wisdom was founded on the timing of his migration, an instinct still wondrously unexplained. The majesty of the high-flying, far-sighted eagle, the terror of all little animals, needs no explanation.

4 God's final challenge

Job 40—41

Once again, the Lord challenges Job to prove himself a worthy opponent in dispute: can he control, let alone create, these two great mythical beasts, Behemoth and Leviathan? 'From the heart of the tempest' (40:6) really gives the answer before we start! In Israel, the intervention of the Lord was always depicted in terms of tempest, storm and earthquake. This idea was perhaps partly inherited from the gods of Canaan, for Baal is the god of the storm, frequently represented in bronze statuettes, hurling the thunderbolt of lightning, often standing on a bull, the emblem of power, life and fertility. The imagery may stem also from the awesome experience of God on the holy mountain of Sinai, when he took Israel to be his very own people. There, amid the stark, majestic scenery of those bare rocks, the whirlwind lightning storms are particularly frightening.

The two mythical beasts, both familiar (at that time) in Egypt, show once again the connection of Israel's Wisdom literature with Egyptian literature. 'Behemoth' is the plural of 'beast, monster'—a sort of plural of majesty or superlative, 'the monster of monsters'—but the description is that of the hippopotamus, a beast not to be trifled with. If you see those great three-toed footprints in the river mud, keep your eyes skinned! If you come upon that long grey back submerged in the water, preceded by those two little eyes, as he 'hides among the reeds in the swamps' (40:21), do not disturb!

The second beast, Leviathan, is a sort of souped-up crocodile. The name indicates a mythical monster of Chaos, a sort of fiery dragon ('from his mouth come fiery torches', 41:11), who features also in Revelation 12:3 as the personification of the evil power of idolatry. The less mythical elements of the description—the double armour of his breastplate, his laughter at a whirring javelin, his daunting rows of teeth, his glittering wake in the water—all fit the crocodile nicely. 'Of all the lordly beasts he is king' (41:26), and the playful description of attempts to bargain with him are all the wittier for that. In blissful ignorance of the danger, I once swam for an hour in the crocodile-infested River Zambesi, to be greeted when I emerged by a chorus of crocodile horror stories.

These two ancient monsters are a fitting pair to conclude the Lord's recital of his achievement in creation.

5 Job's submission

Job 42:1–6

The story has taken a surprising turn. In the earlier exchanges we saw a spirited and pugnacious Job, sarcastic to his 'comforters', outspokenly railing against God, clinging to God but at the same time straining to fling God off his back and decrying the divine bully. Even in his final self-justification, he was aristocratically self-confident, perhaps to the point of arrogance. Now all that has changed, and he meekly submits, even to the point of accusing himself of misrepresenting God by his own ignorant words.

No answers have been given to his questions, but the questions and the bravado alike have vanished. Job's reason? 'Having seen you with my own eyes, I retract' (vv. 5–6). This is obviously not a physical viewing, for 'no human being can see God and live' and there has been no hint of anything so coarse, but, through this parade of divine power and wisdom in creation, Job has been brought to recognize his own weakness and futility. There is no arguing with such a transcendent God. God has been shown to be on an altogether different plane to human beings, and the only true human wisdom (and Job is still wise) is to acknowledge the utter disparity.

What has wrought this transformation? Is it the brilliance with which all these creatures integrate? Is it the wisdom they show in managing their affairs? Is it their beauty and strength, so attractively portrayed by the poetic qualities of the writing? Is it the argument that Job can create nothing at all? Rather than any logical reasoning, it is the impression of God that has been conveyed—not exactly a seeing but certainly an experience of what God is. God has been seen to be so far above human comprehension that logic and argument simply have no place. God is of a different order, and as well might a brute beast attempt to understand the human mind as the human mind try to reason against God. Think of the most 'intelligent' dog, its head cocked on one side, attempting to understand human wit or irony!

Is this a satisfactory answer or is it another example of divine bullying, pulling rank in just the way of which Job had complained? Is it a 'cop-out' on the part of the author that Job should submit so easily? There are certain similarities here to petitionary prayer: we do not really expect God to change his mind. Prayer is more a submission of our needs and desires, and of ourselves too, to the fatherly care of a loving God. Besides seeing that God is far beyond his complaints and arguments, Job has seen the transcendent divine wisdom and love in a way that leaves no room for petty squabbling.

6 Epilogue

Job 42:7–17

The prose section that concludes the book is rather in the vein of 'And they all lived happily ever after', as the three 'comforters' are rebuked for giving a wrong account of the Lord's ways and Job is rewarded with double the amount of possessions that he had before. A few sweeteners are thrown in on top—for example, that his daughters were the most beautiful women in the land and received the same inheritance rights as their brothers. Job himself is rewarded with an exceptionally long life, a couple of decades longer than even 120 years, the standard figure of total completion. We do wonder quite what Job felt when all his 'friends of former times' came flocking back to enjoy a share in his no doubt generous hospitality (v. 11). Well they might give him 'each... a silver coin, and each a gold ring', rather red-faced, we would hope, after their previous desertion and mockery of him in his time of need. It is a slightly lame conclusion after Job's feisty and penetrating self-defence and after the grandeur of the experience of the Lord that brought him satisfaction after his troubles.

Perhaps the most satisfying element is that the Lord compliments Job on having 'spoken about me correctly' (v. 7), by contrast to the 'friends' who had not done so. This may refer simply to Job's reply after the great revelation of the divine wisdom, but does it also refer to Job's earlier courageous battle for the truth, in which he was not afraid to speak out? In this case, the 'friends' are rebuked for their contentment with plati- tudes unworthy of God, and Job is praised for his persevering search for truth. Even when he was impatiently longing to shake off God's tyranny that he might 'have time to swallow his saliva' (see 7:19), he never gave up on God and still paradoxically clung to God in the belief that some- how they were on the same side. Another touching sign of Job's generous forgiveness is that, after all their abuse of him and insistence that he was in the wrong, he is still entrusted with the task of praying for them.

When the Bible was translated into Greek in the second century BC, the atmosphere had changed. Belief in the resurrection had developed sufficiently for the translator to add at the very end, 'It is written that he will rise again with those whom the Lord raises up', an inspiring and comforting conclusion.

Guidelines

The problem of innocent suffering remains an agonizing one. Much of it may be ascribed to human callousness and cruelty, but not all, for the suffering caused by natural disasters and innocent sickness cannot be so shrugged off. Nor can it be dismissed simply as a challenge to human generosity. Written at a time when belief in afterlife was no more than a tremulous and barely perceptible bud, the Hebrew book of Job (without that little final addition in the Greek) can reach only as far as a blind confidence in the overwhelming wisdom and love of God. It cannot see a solution and yet attests to a certainty that there is one. Struggling to burst into flower is the developed belief in an afterlife in God's loving care.

1 AND 2 PETER

Languishing harmlessly at the back end of the New Testament, 1 and 2 Peter are often overlooked in Christian life and reflection. After all, what appeal could books about waiting for the appearing of Christ have for a generation that possesses everything it needs right now?

Then again, what better antidote to comfortable Christianity than a dose of pure New Testament—unadulterated, bracing and inspirational? These words from Peter are a time capsule, packed with bizarre yet strangely precious treasures from an age when the faith of our earliest brothers and sisters was under fire. These words are a time bomb, exploding our leisurely timetables with urgent warnings from a wider world and dispelling our easy caricatures of 'pie in the sky by and by'.

Peter's concern is life: how to live it, how to live it well and how to survive when all is against you. 1 and 2 Peter are lifestyle tracts: the rich doctrine they contain is never presented for its own sake but only and always to form and inform the kind of people we are called to be. In particular, Peter is ever aware that Christians have a life of exile as resident aliens in a world estranged from God (1:1, 17; 2:11; 5:13), and yet it is also a life touched by glory. As Stanley Hauerwas has said, 'God has not promised us safety, but participation in an adventure called the Kingdom. That seems to me to be great news in a world that is literally dying of boredom' (*First Things* 53, 1995).

Bible references are taken from the New Revised Standard Version.

21–27 APRIL

1 A life deferred

1 Peter 1:1–12

Peter was writing from Rome to people he had probably never met, who were dispersed around modern-day Turkey. But one thing he certainly knew: they were beginning to feel the simmering heat of persecution. Peter's opening call is effervescent with praise, but also bold. The

Christian life is a life deferred. It waits, it suffers, it hopes. It does not possess yet, but it will.

We should not overlook this clearly unashamed and glowing 'brochure work' on Peter's part. Like a tour operator sending advance details of a holiday that has already been booked, Peter wants the hearers of this letter to sense the nearness, the greatness, the brightness and brilliance of salvation, almost to reach out and touch it. It is rightfully ours, since we are mercifully chosen by the Father and (literally) 'reborn into hope'—a hope that lives just as the risen Christ lives (v. 3). It is real—rooted in history by the resurrection of Christ and impervious to all forces of decay (v. 4). And it is ready—'ready to be revealed' (v. 5) when the due time comes. Indeed, all we await is the revelation of Jesus Christ himself (v. 7). He is, as it were, waiting in the wings, hidden only by the curtain of history.

The Christian life cannot be lived 'for now', but it is not merely 'for later'. It is life lived now in the light of the future. Audaciously Peter writes of (literally) 'joy unspeakable and glorified' (v. 8) even in the midst of suffering. The word he uses for 'joy' is festal and loud: it is the song after an angel's visit, the leap of a foetus, the tears of a man saved from suicide (Luke 1:44, 46; Acts 16:34). It is joy touched by heaven's music as it streams from the future into the present moment. Peter's hearers have in their hands only hope, but he wants them to know that the God who moves the ages is working behind and beyond their straitened circumstances. Even the very prophets of old have become their servants, and angels their admirers (v. 12). Their life may be deferred, but what a life it is!

What about us? What if we have become so at home in this present ordering of the world that our hope has been obscured and, consequently, our joy dulled? It is not too late, Peter would say: even exiles in the 21st-century United Kingdom have a new birthright of hope. There is a reward waiting even for us, and adventures for the undertaking, as we shall see.

2 A fearful life

1 Peter 1:13–21

Fear is a universal human emotion. The pupils dilate; the pulse quickens; adrenaline rushes; the stomach churns. There is nothing like fear to concentrate the mind. But what place has fear in church? We might fear an overlong sermon or being buttonholed over coffee, but that's about it. Fear is passé. It has the feel of old-time religion and seems theologically bankrupt in this age of feel-good faith.

But Peter would have us live 'in fear' (literally, v. 17), although by this he does not mean fear of human beings (3:6, 14). There is a quality of concentration and sobriety that befits Christian life better than the quietly sozzled repose of the becalmed life. Our minds must be prepared, our senses alert, our desires in check (v. 13). We are to live as asylum seekers ('as foreigners': v. 17, TNIV), temporarily accommodated, travelling light. We are indeed sojourners, but our journey is not 'the journey of life' or 'the road to self-discovery': it is the way of salvation and it is best travelled in circumspection and awe.

Peter works hard in this section to place his hearers in a wider story than that of the world around them. He reminds us that we live in the shadow of a ransom more costly than we can imagine (vv. 18–20) and in the light of a judgment more searching than our familiarity with God might lead us to expect (v. 17). This is no dry doctrine, but a mandate for a life lived between the cross and the throne. This is why God's people will always be strangers and aliens in a world at war with God. This story will always impel us to live differently from those around us. We will always stick out—but there is a purpose even in this. Karl Barth wrote, 'The church exists… to set up in the world a new sign which is radically dissimilar to [the world's] own manner and which contradicts it in a way which is full of promise' (*Church Dogmatics*, 4.3.2).

If you're anything like me, you won't often think of being judged by a holy God, but Peter considered this idea worth keeping in mind. It motivates us to be different from the world around us, so that church is not just another place to park our cars at the weekend but the genuine sign of a reality yet to come.

3 A shared life

1 Peter 1:22—2:10

There are 60 reasons to leave church: the loss of a loved one, a crisis of faith, a new house, new hobby, pressure at work, a fall-out, the loss of cherished services, a callous minister, ill health, boredom, a sense of gradual exclusion and so on. There are 60 reasons to leave church but one reason to stay: the gospel of Jesus Christ.

The gospel goes deeper. The good news of Christ cannot remain at the level of the shallow and the temporary. The 'word of God' (the gospel) does not wither or perish. It lives; it endures (1:23). As we grow in our salvation, so the gospel works deeper into our system, drilling down beneath surface appearances to the very core of our relationships. You began by love and obedience, Peter points out (1:22); now let that love permeate your heart and cast out all sub-Christian ways of relating to each other. Notice how clearly he focuses on relationships in 1:22 and 2:1. God's children must learn to love beyond superficiality and distrust. Church is the school of that genuine love it should be the place where we taste a love like no other; it may also be the place where our ability to love is stretched to the limit.

The gospel builds something greater. To come to Christ is to be built together with others into a greater whole. The church has a purpose larger than the adding of individual names to a list. It has a jubilant, ongoing, praise-giving function: 'to proclaim the mighty acts' of God (2:9). Our great honour is to join in. Ultimately, Peter invites his readers to be bold enough to see that we (yes, even we!) have become the very people of God, with all their privileges and responsibilities (2:9–11). We may have thought our conversion was just a personal step of faith, but all the time God was busily grafting us into the renewed and regal people of Israel. Indeed, what other way could there be for us to be saved? To seek salvation without joining God's people would be like requesting an individual Red Sea boat pass rather than following in the footsteps of Moses.

Church may often be difficult, but how else can we live the shared life described in these verses? How can we form a temple together unless we learn to lean on each other? Can a house be made of one brick?

4 A good life

For an activity that involves being nice, 'do gooding' has a pretty bad name. It is associated with ostentatious charity, unwanted help or (worst of all) 'works righteousness'. But the doing of good is precisely what Peter is after: 'honourable deeds', 'doing right', 'live for righteousness', and so on.

Behind Peter's thought, especially this extended treatment of the Christian's place in society, is the thought of a cycle. He sees a negative spiral at work in all areas of life: evil begets evil; insult breeds insult; abuse at work causes resentment; overbearing husbands and distracted wives gradually lose respect for one another; long-running tensions can turn church into a nest of bitterness. We have all felt the rough end of this cycle at one time or other. How hard it is, when we are mistreated, to do anything but reply in kind! Peter fears that his hearers, maligned and mistreated as they are, might get sucked into this meaningless spiral of malice and recrimination. It is time for the cycle to stop, he says, and it must stop with us (3:9).

Why and how can we break the cycle? Because of Jesus. At his passion, he plunged into the heart of its violence and retributive anger. He let the cycle do its worst, but refused to retaliate. He felt the full force of evil in his body, but never lost sight of the guilty 'other' whom he sought to save (2:22–24). Having broken the rules of the cycle in his death, Christ then shattered the cycle itself in his resurrection and broke its power to enslave. This is the cross set forth in a stirring, vital way. Christ's death was not just an extreme sacrificial measure, but a powerful, moral, in-spirational act—an act of insubordination to the powers of evil and their cycle of sin.

Now Christ's journey is ours—the footsteps we are called to follow (2:21). Now we too must break the cycle of evil that threatens to destroy our very souls (2:11). Now it is ours to say, 'I will not be just another disgruntled employee… just another casually thoughtless husband or glittering, distracted wife… just another self-righteous tax dodger or quietly malicious church member. In Christ, I can break the cycle. He has set me free and now I will serve God with all the intoxicating liberty that comes with being enabled to do good.'

5 A public life

To go public as a Christian is to risk ridicule, isolation and suspicion. This was certainly Tony Blair's experience on several occasions when his faith surfaced in the media, such as when Jeremy Paxman asked him sneeringly if he prayed with George Bush (*Newsnight*, 6 Feb 2003). It would be easy to become intimidated (v. 14), and yet Christian faith remains inescapably public.

Firstly, Christians are committed to public actions. Peter continues to commend good deeds, even in the face of suffering (vv. 13–14, 16–17). Not only is contribution to the greater good the necessary overflow of a heart devoted to God's will, but it may also have an effect on those around us, whether to win them (2:12) or to silence them (3:16). Secondly, Christians are committed to public words. When lives shaped by hope provoke questions or challenges, a 'defence' will be needed (v. 15). We cannot avoid the command to speak. If we sanctify Christ as Lord in our hearts, he will not stay there. Again, the temptation to fear is great—or to overcompensate with thick-skinned arrogance. But Peter is aware of this, and thus extols a careful dance of courage and gentleness (vv. 14, 16).

Peter then develops a deeper theme: a profound confidence wrapped up in mysterious imagery (vv. 18–22). Christ is our example in suffering for righteousness, but also, in his resurrection, he has become the promise of something greater. Peter envisions the risen Christ traversing spiritual planes, confronting malevolent forces and then taking his place at the right hand of God. The time of the flood was infamous for its rebellion and chaos, so much so that only a few could be saved. But Peter sees Christ as announcing his glorious victory to the very spirits responsible for those godless times (according to Jewish tradition, such spirits had been imprisoned, awaiting God's judgment). If the risen Christ is Lord even over these spirits, even over the darkest eras in human history, then surely he is above all powers and authorities (v. 22), and that same risen Messiah has now saved us through baptism. No wonder we are not to fear!

Christianity is not, and never can be, private. The baptism that saves us cannot be administered internally(!) but only as a drenching of our body before others. Such a life before others may cause us to quake, but Peter would remind us that if the Lord of our hearts is also the Lord of the

127

universe, then his presence can drive out any fear, whatever those around us may say.

6 A costly life

1 Peter 4:1–11

'The reason many are still troubled, still seeking, still making little forward progress,' said A.W. Tozer, 'is because they haven't come to the end of themselves.' In yet another reflection on the cross, Peter sees in Christ's death a refusal to capitulate to sin, no matter what the cost (vv. 1–2). If we are to follow Christ, we too must come to a kind of breaking point. We must come to the end of ourselves and determine to live the rest of our earthly lives for the will of God. We must take up arms ('arm yourselves', v. 1) against sin's tyranny and end our entanglement in its affairs.

The first application of this costly discipleship is disengagement from the unbridled excesses of pagan culture (vv. 3–6). Peter has in mind abusive and addictive patterns of sex, drugs and entertainment, but by extension he implies that we should break our truce with any unrestrained appetites, cherished addictions or debilitating habits.

There is also a more subtle cost of discipleship—not a solitary act of valour or a stunning personal reformation, but a series of disciplines for the life shaped by love. Alertness and prayer (v. 7) require us to displace treasured routines, either of leisurely inconsistency or frenetic hurry. Forgiveness (v. 8) consists, in effect, of paying the debts others owe to us, covering their sins with our love. Hospitality (v. 9) allows others to invade spaces we are used to keeping to ourselves. Serving one another (vv. 10–11) also requires a step of faith in the words that only God can give, the strength only he supplies.

Do we do these things? Do we forgive, serve and welcome beyond the breaking point of cost, or do we stop short of it? Peter would have us push through: through the barriers of inconvenience and social respectability to the point where our resources end and God's begin. As Roy Hession wrote, 'Every humiliation, everyone who tries and vexes us, is God's way of breaking us, so that there is yet a deeper channel in us for the life of Christ' (*The Calvary Road*, CLC, 1950, p. 15). The heart falters at such points, and the knees weaken, but these breaking points will be the making of us and a moment of encounter with the lavish provision of God, to his greater glory (v. 11).

Guidelines

Look back over the readings so far. Where has Peter challenged or inspired you in your lifestyle? What would it mean to walk in this challenge or inspiration? In the spirit of a shared life, why not share these insights with a friend somehow?

1 A blessed life

1 Peter 4:12–19

'Do not be surprised,' writes Peter. Surprised? How about downright perplexed? Joy in sufferings, blessings in curses, and God judging his own Church? This is Christianity from another planet! But it is here that Peter's themes—our exile in the world, the imitation of Christ, the promise of glory—come to full expression as he deals with suffering head on.

God would have for himself a people tested and approved through the crucible of adversity (v. 12). Those who suffer for Christ are close to him, sharing his sufferings; and he is close to them through a glory in advance—the Spirit of God resting upon them (vv. 13–14). The thorns and thistles of a fallen world made a crown for Christ; they will leave their mark on all who confront sin's world in his footsteps.

Deeper still, there is a brooding apocalyptic sense here. God's end time judgment—'the mighty hand of God' (5:6)—is coming. It cannot be stopped, and its purifying work begins at 'the household of God' (4:17). To be a Christian is not to escape all suffering. It is to face, willingly and with Christ, the refining fire of God and the costs of a broken world, rather than to face these realities without Christ on the day of judgment.

But what do we know of this? What do we know, who carp at a boring sermon or falter at church services not to our taste? At this point we must be silent. On ground hallowed by the suffering of others, we must listen humbly and allow them to interpret this scripture for us. One such example is Brother Samuel, who converted to Christianity from Islam but was arrested by a Middle Eastern government and tortured, including three months' confinement in a stone box. He said this:

I was just a wreck in that cell… Crying, weeping, sobbing, wailing in the never changing utter darkness. I came face to face with how awful I really was… But just as I was about to collapse into complete despair and self-loathing—and probably die—an incredible realization burst into the cell like an exploding star. It was this: Jesus loved me even right then, as I sat in my own filth, weak, helpless, broken, empty, sinful. Even in that state, he loved me! And Christ rushed in and filled me, and the filling was so great because I was so empty.

RONALD BOYD-MACMILLAN, 'PREACHING THE LOVE OF ONE'S ENEMIES', ANVIL, VOL. 22, No 1, 2005, P. 20

2 A contested life

1 Peter 5:1–14

'Today's church suffers from suffocating niceness,' wrote Stanley Hauerwas (*Resident Aliens*, Abingdon Press, 1989, p. 149). Today we have no enemies. We are a peacetime church, and in peacetime we can absorb ourselves in personal fulfilment, private ambitions and the occasional internal soap opera.

Peter's church was not at peace. Peter's church sojourned in a world where every step was opposed by the powers of evil. This leads me to conclude that either the nature of evil has radically changed or somehow we have become deadened to the contested life of the people of God.

The church faces institutional danger. As its appointed shepherds attempt to lead the flock from the front, they must face the temptations of demotivation, greed and self-importance (vv. 1–4). Meanwhile, the rest of the church will need to beware of arrogance and a rebellious spirit (v. 5). We are also in constant spiritual danger from pride and worry

(vv. 6–7). Contrary to present-day fashions in spirituality, Peter warns us sharply that behind these attacks lies a personal demonic force that seeks nothing less than our physical and spiritual destruction (v. 8). Finally there is the ominous threat of worldly opposition. This letter comes to us from a coded place—'Babylon' (v. 13), that is, Rome—reminding us of the ongoing clash of values between Caesar's empire and God's kingdom.

How can we live well in contested times? A key is in verse 8. We need the clear-headed concentration that Peter has recommended through-out this epistle. We must also come to terms (or, rather, not come to terms) with Satan. Peter is emphatic that this dark figure lies behind our conceits and rivalries, our anxieties and distracted lives. Firstly, we must 'keep alert'—not seeking demons under stones but recognizing who stands to benefit when we fall captive to sin (Ephesians 4:27). Secondly, we need to be proactive in areas where we have become entangled: 'humble yourselves', 'cast all your anxiety', 'resist him', 'stand fast'. Finally, we need to trust in God's power to 'deliver us from the evil one' (Matthew 6:13, TNIV). He is, after all, 'the God of all grace' and his resources are more than sufficient to bring us to journey's end (vv. 10–11). With that in mind, even in the midst of the contest, we can know 'peace' (v. 14).

3 Attention to life

2 Peter 1:1–15

In 2 Peter, the apostle speaks to us from beyond the grave (though whether it is Peter's own final testimony or reflections gathered by a follower is hard to establish). As an old man, Peter's great enemy is forgetfulness—not his own, but ours. We must not forget (v. 9); we must let him remind us (v. 12), refresh our memory (v. 13), help us to recall (v. 15). Recall what? The value of our inheritance. We have been given a 'precious' faith (v. 1), and 'precious and very great promises' (v. 4). Peter's concern is that we should appreciate the worth of the family heirloom, that we forget neither the gift of salvation nor what it takes to inherit it.

He begins with the profound confidence that we have seen before.

God has made a way for 'life and godliness' (v. 3), but salvation still takes the form of an inheritance—promises yet to be received, a calling still to be fulfilled. God has made a way, but there remains the tragic possibility that some might stumble from it (v. 10).

Peter does not suggest that we provide or maintain our place in the kingdom by our own power, but his admonition here is crystal clear: 'make every effort', 'confirm your call', 'if you do this, you will never stumble'. Only if we let God's power go to work in every area of our lives over time (our morality, our mentality, our durability, our community life and so on) will we gain entry into Christ's kingdom. If I had preached like this at training college, I might have been docked marks for gracelessness and/or poor theology. The only marks Peter wanted, however, were the marks of discipleship. He well remembered Jesus' command: 'Make every effort to enter through the narrow door' (Luke 13:24, NIV). This is why Dietrich Bonhoeffer told his seminarians that prayer must not take flight 'from the most important thing: prayer for our own soul's salvation' (*Meditating on the Word*, Cowley Publications, 1986, p. 33).

The church today chases all kinds of 'fruitfulness', be it larger numbers, greater miracles or worthier projects, but Peter cared most about the quality and longevity of Christian life (v. 8). Like a pearl diver, he was looking for the fully formed gem. Is the treasure of the gospel in our own lives of the same value to us?

4 Attention to scripture

2 Peter 1:16–21

I wonder whether the original author of these words would have appreciated the irony. Here is one of the staunchest defences of biblical reliability in the whole of scripture, and yet it appears in a book whose authorship has been more disputed than almost any other!

The letters of 1 and 2 Peter contain plenty of human fingerprints. There are unclear verses. There is the influence of Peter's scribe, Silvanus (1 Peter 5:12). There is wholesale borrowing from other books (2 Peter 2 is probably lifted from Jude, which in turn drew from the non-scriptural book of 1 Enoch). There are signs of underlying theological tension (not least the question of apostasy raised in our previous passage). There is an open challenge to the perspicuity of scripture, when Peter admits that some of Paul's writings are 'hard to understand' (2 Peter 3:16). And then there is the occasional puzzle as to which Greek manuscript is original: for instance, we need to judge between at least four different options for 2 Peter 3:10.

Presumably, the fact that the authors of apostolic documents were human wasn't news to the writer of 2 Peter. Yet he also calls our bluff. If the apostle's testimony about Jesus Christ is not true, it is a 'myth' (v. 16), and Peter himself repudiates that idea. Either the prophetic word is a lamp (v. 19) or we remain in the darkness—for what other light could we have by which to judge? Either prophecy originates in the purposes of the God who speaks or merely in the imagination of an oracle (v. 21). Yes, we navigate a dark place where not all is illumined; yes, prophecy is a lamp, not the morning star itself; yes, it was real men and women who spoke. But they spoke from God, and somehow the Holy Spirit carried them along. Without this fact, we have no compass.

As it is, the apostles' actual historical experience of the transfiguration functions as a pledge of what is to come: 'the power and coming of our Lord Jesus Christ' (v. 16). The transfiguration was the movie trailer—showing a glimpse of the film in advance, so that we might be sure that the full feature is on its way. It is because they saw his glory then that we can know that God's Messiah is reigning now, and will one day claim his entire creation. If the Church ceases to witness to this truth, it loses its function.

5 Attention to judgment

2 Peter 2

Peter's diatribe against these teachers probably sounds very harsh to our ears. We should perhaps consider, though, how we react to news of fraudulent quacks selling fake 'medicines' to those dying of AIDS, or ruthless acts of violence on our streets that destroy the lives of innocent people. We tend to save our righteous indignation for matters of health and safety while applying tolerance to all things religious. But Peter saw in the wake of these false teachers a trail of destruction as wanton and cruel as any we might care to imagine, undoing the good work of God, wasting the lives of misguided converts and squandering many people's eternity along the way.

What might we learn from Peter's words? For one thing, he has a clear concept of orthodox Christian teaching (v. 1), and how important it is to submit to it (v. 10). In particular, he insists on the doctrine of a coming judgment that takes account of our deeds. Without this anchor, the lives of both teachers and hearers begin to drift. Notice that Peter is not embarrassed by the judgment of God or the Old Testament passages that demonstrate it. Christ has not replaced the judgment of God with an all-embracing acceptance; rather, through him we 'escape' the world's corruption and the judgment it precipitates (1:4; 2:20). God is Saviour, and yet still also Judge. For this reason our actions, both good and bad, continue to count.

What drives Peter, though, is not judgment as such, but the wonder of grace. It is because there is a 'Master who bought them' (v. 1) that the false prophets' apostasy is so hurtful. It is because there really is a 'way of truth' that those who disgrace it are so toxic (v. 2). Appalled by corrupt and negligent teachers, Peter sets out a vision for the Christian life that is truly breathtaking: we are not to be mastered by anything (v. 19); we are not to be 'entangled' or 'overpowered' by the world's corruption (vv. 19–20). We are free in the most glorious and godly way, and Peter expects all Christians to know this freedom.

It is in the light of this wonderful, world-saving truth that false teachers must be opposed, even 'with tears' (Philippians 3:18). Is this truth not worth standing up for? Provided we use only 'the weapons of righteousness' (2 Corinthians 6:7), is it not worth fighting for?

6 Attention to hope

2 Peter 3

We live in a society in which hope has collapsed, to be replaced with the prefabricated structures of individual life-fulfilment. The church, too, is still emerging from a long season marked by the loss of confidence in the coming of Christ. Scholars, unmindful of Peter's words here, once high-mindedly declared that two thousand years is too long for a coming initially described as 'soon'. Two thousand years is two days, claims Peter (v. 8)—barely the wait from Good Friday to Easter Sunday.

Why is it so hard to believe in the appearing of Jesus Christ? Perhaps because everything around us feels so solid and unchanging. Yet Peter's logic in verses 5–7 still carries weight. Where did reality come from? A universe that exists at all suggests the existence of a power great enough to conceive and constantly sustain it. But if this is the case, then the universe also suggests a power great enough one day to purge and renew it. Cannot the God who created by a word also conclude by a word (v. 5)?

What will happen at that time? Certainly the mother of all conflagrations (v. 10). The heavens, the 'elements', godlessness and the godless will all be destroyed with 'a loud noise' (which is presumably like a youth worship band, only worse!). Peter deliberately adopts language and imagery big enough to make us reconsider the whole of our lives in the light of this coming day (v. 11).

However, the fires of judgment will not lead to the earth and everything that is done on it being 'burned up' (v. 10, KJV, reflecting a later manuscript of 2 Peter). Instead, they will be 'disclosed' (NRSV, literally 'found'). The earth and its history will be found—found like the life lost for Christ is found (Matthew 10:39); found like a coin sought with tears (Luke 15:8); found as we ourselves will be found (v. 14, even through fire, 1 Peter 1:7). After all, the result of God's saving promise is not 'no heavens and no earth', but 'new heavens and a new earth' (v. 13).

The balance of Christian living is therefore to live our lives here in exile in such a way that we are not 'at home', yet also to walk with the faithful Creator and work the kind of righteousness that will one day be at home. The final sting in the tail here is that it may well be us that God is waiting for. 'He is patient with you,' writes Peter (v. 9), suggesting that God waits even now for us, the people of God, to hasten his coming by bringing our lives into greater alignment with Peter's words.

Guidelines

'I live for two days: today and that day,' wrote Martin Luther. Spend some time reflecting on the coming day of judgment, remembering the grace of salvation but also the responsibilities it brings.

FURTHER READING

Richard J. Bauckham, *Jude, 2 Peter*, Word, 1983.

Stanley Hauerwas and William H. Willimon, *Resident Aliens*, Abingdon Press, 1989.

I.H. Marshall, *1 Peter*, IVP, 1991.

The BRF

Magazine

Richard Fisher writes...

'Pray as you can, not as you can't.' What could be simpler than talking to God? Yet so many Christians say that they find prayer a very difficult part of Christian life. Perhaps it's because there is usually no immediate response to our prayers, no way of knowing whether we've 'got it right' or not.

There is much in the world around us and in our own thoughts and feelings that we can turn into prayer, with a little encouragement. In this issue of the *BRF Magazine*, David Winter shows us how we can follow the example of the psalmists who expressed their changing emotions—positive and negative—to God with complete openness and honesty.

Then, in an extract from Joyce Huggett's prayer anthology, *Embracing God's World* (first published in 1996), we find inspiration for prayers of thanksgiving towards the Creator of the natural world. Not all of us can respond to the beauties of creation with the poetic fluency of Joyce's prayers, but another way of praying featured in the Magazine is simple enough for us all. In this issue, Naomi Starkey recommends *The Jesus Prayer*, another popular book being reprinted this year. In this book, Bishop Simon Barrington-Ward explains the past and present use of this ancient ten-word prayer: 'Lord Jesus Christ, Son of God, have mercy on me.'

At the end of the Magazine, you'll find another simple 'formula' for prayer, based on the four fingers and thumb of one hand—an idea from our *Barnabas* website that could prove a useful aid for children and adults alike. But before that, in an extract from our prayer and spirituality magazine, *Quiet Spaces*, Ann Persson meditates on the real purpose of prayer—to open ourselves up to God and his work in our lives.

BRF is committed to helping you to pray. Whether you recite other people's prayers or make up your own, whether you take your inspiration from the physical world or from your own emotions, our extract from David Winter's latest BRF book, *Journey to Jerusalem*, reminds us that we are speaking to Abba—the Father who loves us, understands all our human experiences and longs to hear us pray, in whatever way we can.

Richard Fisher, Chief Executiv

Prayer: inspired by the Psalms

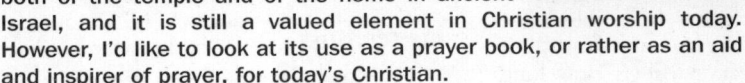

David Winter

'None ever came up dry from David's well,' wrote the 18th-century preacher Matthew Henry. 'David's well' was, of course, the Psalter, which we call the 'Psalms of David'. It was the hymn book both of the temple and of the home in ancient Israel, and it is still a valued element in Christian worship today. However, I'd like to look at its use as a prayer book, or rather as an aid and inspirer of prayer, for today's Christian.

The first thing that strikes anyone browsing through the Psalms is their stunning honesty. Here no holds are barred. If the psalmist is angry with God or frustrated at God's apparent reluctance to answer his prayers, he says so—and in the most direct, even fierce language. If, on the other hand, the psalmist is angry with someone else, either those frequently described as his 'enemies' or, worse still, those he sees as God's enemies, then vengeance of the most terrible kind may be called for. If the psalmist is frightened or ill, or feels abandoned, he is utterly open about it. These writers are not ones to mince words! If God is as great and his mercy ('loving-kindness', in the beautiful language of the King James Version) as inexhaustible as the psalmists believe them to be, then their cries, even of anger, will reach his ears and evoke a merciful response. The Psalms tell us that what God wants above everything else in our prayers is absolute honesty. We need to tell it the way it is.

With those thoughts in mind, we might look at some of the psalms and see the ways in which they can prompt and inspire our prayers today. Three thousand years don't seem to have changed human nature or human needs, and they certainly haven't changed the nature or character of God.

> *These writers are not ones to mince words*

Days of spiritual dryness

Several psalms seem to arise from a situation that most believers are familiar with—what might be called 'spiritual dryness' or, more dramatically, the 'dark night of the soul'. The God we thought we knew and have been in constant touch with suddenly seems remote—indeed, deaf to our cries and silent in response to our prayers. Psalm 13:1 catches both the condition and the frustration very vividly: 'How long, O Lord? Will you forget me forever? How long will you hide your face from me?' (NRSV). The psalmist is utterly open about his feelings: 'I bear pain in my soul… sorrow in my heart all day long' (v. 2).

This is not by any means the only psalm to express this kind of disappointment. Psalm 22 is, if anything, even more desperate. The writer feels forsaken, with God far distant and deaf to 'the words of my groaning' (v. 2). Others (Psalms 28, 38 and 69, for instance) have the same theme. The God in whom the writers have trusted seems to have withdrawn. In a time of need, their cries are simply not being heard.

Yet each of these psalms eventually offers exactly the same answer to the dilemma. It is not God who has changed: how could he? After all, his love is 'steadfast'. The psalmists have known his faithfulness all through their lives. Indeed, their ancestors trusted in him and he delivered them (22:4). So if it is not God who has changed, then the problem lies within the soul of the psalmist himself. Faith must be rekindled, the gifts and goodness of the Lord recalled and celebrated. Look how Psalm 13 ends: 'I trusted in your steadfast love; my heart shall rejoice in your salvation' (v. 5).

The psalmist is utterly open about his feelings

The key word in each of these psalms is the tiny preposition 'but'. Just read them, and you will see how crucial it is. We feel abandoned, *but* we are not!

In time of illness

It's often hard to pray when we are ill, partly because of physical discomfort or pain and partly because we may be overwhelmed by anxiety or fear. Many will have shared the experience of Psalm 77—the inability to sleep because of anxiety and sorrow. If so, Psalm 6 might be a good starting place, because the writer is quite open and honest about both experiences. He has one terror, however, that should be spared the Christian believer: there was no clear belief in life beyond death at that time, which accounts for the negative message of verse 5.

Nevertheless, once again the psalm ends with a clear note of hope. His illness was not a punishment sent by God, and his prayers and tears have not gone unnoticed. 'The Lord has heard the sound of my weeping. The Lord has heard my supplication; the Lord accepts my prayer' (vv. 8–9). His faith may have failed, but God's faithfulness has not.

Joy and contentment

Just as often as the psalmist reflects on his problems and difficulties, he (or, as I shall suggest, possibly she!) bursts into praise and worship. This, too, can inspire our own prayers because, while gratitude is spontaneous, it is wonderfully enriching to find beautiful words and images to express our moments of joy. Psalm 103 is the classic hymn of praise ('Bless the Lord, O my soul, and all that is within me, bless his holy name': v. 1). Psalm 84 captures in beautiful poetry the security and contentment of trust: 'How lovely is your dwelling place, O Lord of hosts! … Happy are those whose strength is in you… A day in your courts is better than a thousand elsewhere' (vv. 1, 5, 10).

For me, however, one short psalm (131) captures the contentment of faith perfectly. The imagery employed suggests to me that the author must have been a woman: 'I have calmed and quieted my soul, like a weaned child with its mother; my soul is like the weaned child that is with me' (v. 2). It also has a touching modesty and reticence about it—not exactly a hallmark of most of the psalms: 'O Lord, my heart is not lifted up, my eyes are not raised too high; I do not occupy myself with things too great and too marvellous for me' (v. 1). 'O Israel,' it ends, 'hope in the Lord from this time on and forevermore' (v. 3). Amen!

David Winter is an honorary Canon of Christ Church, Oxford, a regular contributor to New Daylight *Bible reading notes and a Series Editor of* The People's Bible Commentary.

For further study on the Psalms, *The People's Bible Commentary* offers two volumes, both written by former Archbishop of Canterbury, Donald Coggan. To order copies, please turn to the order form on page 159.

An extract from
Embracing God's World

Embracing God's World—a revised edition of a collection first published in 1996—brings together Joyce Huggett's personal selection of prayers new and old. The prayers printed here, all written by Joyce herself, are expressions of thanksgiving and adoration inspired by the natural world.

Hallelujah! Christ is risen!

I saw you in the fullness of the moon
that lighted my path
on the way to the tomb.
I saw you in the dove-shaped cloud
that hovered over the hills
as we waited for sunrise.
I saw you in the sun which
slid over the mountain
in all its majesty—
thrilling us with its appearance.
I saw you in the liquid gold cross
traced on the sea
by the rays of the rising sun.

I worshipped you
in the strains of the aria from Handel's Messiah
that heralded that sunrise:
'I know that my Redeemer lives...'

I heard and felt you when,
like the angel,
I sat outside the garden tomb
and wanted to shriek:
'He is not here... he is risen!'

Joy. Pure joy.

Was it you?

Someone smudged the sky with pink
    this morning, Lord.
Was it you?

Someone even painted the sea pink.
Was that you?

No camera could capture
    the mystery,
        the majesty,
            the magic
of those flamingo pink
    smears and smudges and streaks
        mingling with the cloudless blue
            of a winter's sky.
No paintbrush could colour the sea
    salmon pink.
It must have been you.

Someone filled the air
    with birdsong this morning, Lord.
Was it you?
Did you set the cockerels crowing,
    the robins warbling ,
        the sparrows twittering,
            the great-tits singing 'pink-pink', 'see-saw'?
No human visionary could dream up the dawn chorus.
It must have been you.

Sunset

One part of the sky
seemed like a frothing, foaming sea tonight, Lord—
not white suds
but swirls of pink
tinged with purple.
Across the steel blue of a cloudless patch of sky
someone seemed to be stretching streamers—
fluorescent pink that changed before my eyes
from pink to vermilion to purple.
Cars rushed by—
occupants oblivious of the pageant in the sky—
while I stood riveted,
awed,
transfixed by the grandeur.
Was it colour like this that prompted the psalmist to sing:
'The heavens declare the glory of God'?
As now, so then, did you throw open
the casements of heaven and allow him to gaze on
your beauty,
your majesty,
your magnificence,
your splendour?
Who can tell?
For beckoning me from my desk
and thrilling me afresh with this glimpse of your glory,
I give you humble and heartfelt thanks.

Raindrops

Raindrops dangling
*   like bright baubles*
*   on the fronds of the bottle-brush tree.*
Enjoy them.

To order a copy of *Embracing God's World*, please turn to the order form on page 159.

Lent book 2008:
Journey to Jerusalem

This new book by David Winter (BRF's Lent book for 2008) follows the journey of Jesus and his followers to Jerusalem—where his ministry will culminate in the events of Good Friday and Easter. As we reflect on these events, like the disciples we can experience the awakening of faith in Jesus and hear the challenge to follow him, wherever he leads. With them we can tread the path to Gethsemane and Golgotha, and on to the empty tomb and new life. The following abridged extracts are taken from the Introduction and the reading for Day 37, 'The place of prayer'.

Introduction

It was the 15th year of the reign of the emperor Tiberius—about AD27 in our calendar. He chose to spend many months of the year at his palace on the southern headland of the beautiful island of Capri, overlooking the blue waters swirling below. He probably felt rather pleased with himself. His empire was, relatively speaking, at peace—a peace enforced by a splendid system of law and the most finely trained and equipped (and, when necessary, ruthless) army in human history…

There had never been an empire quite like this. Its architects and engineers built roads, aqueducts, theatres and arenas. Its lawyers, orators and judges administered the law. Having largely absorbed the culture of Greece, more and more people were educated and sophisticated. The Senate and the tribunes of the people were there, in principle at least, in the interests of a kind of democracy. Yes, Tiberius could justifiably feel that he was ruler of an empire that would last for ever.

As he hunted the wild boar on Capri, far away to the east in a remote and troublesome province of his empire twelve young men were walking with their leader along a road near Caesarea Philippi. They were about 30 miles north of Galilee, in a hilly area where the river Jordan had its source. As they walked, their leader put two questions to them, and the answer to the second one would have profound consequences not just for them but for the future of Tiberius' empire and eventually the whole world.

The leader was Jesus. The twelve young men (and they were young, most of them barely in their 20s) were his disciples.

This story begins with those questions and the disciples' answers to them, and then traces the dramatic and painful consequences of that conversation on the road. The conversation itself would eventually set them on the path to Jerusalem, where the enemies of Jesus were waiting to pounce on the unorthodox young prophet from Galilee. It set in train a sequence of events which we shall see as three acts of a great drama—a drama that encompassed all the fundamental themes of every tragic story and every tale of triumph ever told. It included a quest, as many great stories do, but the quest was not for personal glory, wealth or the hand of a beautiful princess. It was a story of 'rags to riches', as the son of a carpenter from the obscure and sometimes ridiculed village of Nazareth changed the history of the world so profoundly that its most common calendar was to be measured in terms of years before or after his coming. It was a story of opposition overcome, of a dark and malign power to be faced, of tragedy and—ultimately—of triumph...

That story, those events and the group of disciples slowly making their way southwards towards Jerusalem will be the subjects of our Lenten reflection.

The place of prayer

Read Mark 14:32–41.

Key verse: 'Abba, Father, for you all things are possible; remove this cup from me; yet, not what I want, but what you want' (v. 36).

From the upper room, Jesus and the disciples probably made their way through the temple courts, across the Kidron valley and then up the path towards the Mount of Olives. There they came to a garden, one that Jesus had obviously used before as a place of prayer. It was called Gethsemane, which means 'wine press', and it was more like an orchard than a garden, filled with olive trees. It still is today, as many a pilgrim to Jerusalem can testify.

It had been a strange evening, which the eleven disciples would certainly never forget. This had been a Passover meal like no other they had experienced, and now they had made their way from the warmth of the room through the fresh, cool air of an April evening to this lonely venue. Unusually, Mark has the fullest account of what happened there, with several details not recorded in the other Gospels. He notes that when they arrived Jesus seemed 'distressed and agitated' (14:33)—'deeply grieved, even to death' (v. 34). The quiet garden at this late hour was to be the scene of one of the most heart-rending prayers ever uttered, one of the most shocking betrayals and one of the most cowardly mass desertions in the history of religion. Here was a place of high drama indeed, a moment in which we can see the horror of Jesus the man struggling with the destiny of Jesus the Son of God.

When they arrived, Jesus suggested to the rest of the disciples that they spent time in prayer while he himself moved on a little way into the trees with Peter, James and John. It was with them that he shared his own state of mind, his spiritual turmoil and agitation. Then, asking them to stay awake and pray, he moved on a further few paces and threw himself on the ground, a position identified with the most intense kind of intercession. The subject of his prayer is summarized by Mark in disarmingly simple words: he 'prayed that, if it were possible, the hour might pass from him' (v. 35). This 'hour' was the simplest available Greek word for 'time', yet one that could also carry the meaning of a due time or a moment of destiny…

Jesus' prayer continued, presumably overheard by the three disciples: 'Abba, Father, for you all things are possible.' They had heard that phrase on his lips before—'for God all things are possible'—but in that earlier situation he had been talking of the possibility that even a rich person might be saved (Mark 10:27). Here, to their astonishment, he was speaking of something infinitely more mysterious, an alteration to the working out of God's purposes through his chosen Messiah. 'Remove this cup from me': the request was simple, at one level. The cup, as the disciples would have known, was the bitter cup of suffering—even, perhaps, the cup that holds the wrath of God against sin (Jeremiah 25:15). But, if everything is possible for God, why couldn't he find a less shameful and brutal way for the world's salvation to be won? Could there not be a less horrible 'plan B'?

Could there not be a less horrible 'plan B'?

There is a tendency for Christians reading the Gospels to view them so exclusively through the lens of the resurrection that they miss the reality of the horror that faced Jesus at this point. We know that he is the Son of God. We know that God raised him from the dead. We know that the suffering and death ahead of him were part of God's purposes of love, the means by which healing and forgiveness would become available to the entire human race. With all that in mind, we might tend to think of Christ's suffering and death as elements in a kind of cosmic drama rather than the actual experiences of a flesh-and-blood man…

Jesus of Nazareth was fully human. It would be a grievous misunderstanding of the incarnation if it were not so. The Son of Man was also, of course, the Son of God: that is the clear teaching of the New Testament. In him the two natures were both fully present. As a man, Jesus looked at what lay ahead and was appalled. His body would be assaulted, scourged and beaten. Nails would be driven through his wrists. Hanging on the cross, his internal organs would be ruptured. Finally, in the heat of the afternoon, he would die. It's hard to see anything in that prospect to evoke cheerfulness.

Yet because he was also the Son of God, the prayer in the garden didn't end there. It went on, 'Yet, not what I want, but what you want' (Mark 14:36). Even in the face of the most appalling suffering, rejection and death, with all the mysterious consequences of dying for the sins of the world and the temporary but real severing of the eternal relationship of intimacy with his Father that death would entail, the divine will and purpose that Jesus had set himself to follow remained paramount in his intentions. 'I seek to do not my own will, but the will of him who sent me' (John 5:30): that had been the benchmark of his whole ministry. Now it faced its sternest test, but the Messiah did not fail.

Jesus didn't want to be scourged and beaten, crucified and killed. If that sounds obvious, it probably still needs to be said. If it sounds shocking or even blasphemous, then we have not fully taken on board the meaning of the incarnation. The issue for Jesus in the garden was to set aside his own wishes, fears and feelings as a man, in order to fulfil the will of his Father… There in the garden of Gethsemane the struggle was short-lived, because both the Father and the Son knew that the outcome of the suffering would be healing for the nations.

The spiritual test was over. Exhausted—his sweat, Luke tells us, like 'great drops of blood' (22:44)—he went to find his friends in the darkness. Urged to stay awake and pray, at the moment of his greatest need they had fallen asleep.

A reflection

Mark, alone of the Gospel writers, tells us that the prayer of Jesus was addressed to 'Abba', the Aramaic name of intimacy for a father… When Jesus cried out in his agony, his prayer was not addressed to a remote creative force, or to some implacable and unmovable higher power, but to his 'Father in heaven'. So may ours be, in our moments of agony and sorrow. We can come as children to a loving heavenly Father—Abba.

To order a copy of this book, please turn to the order form on page 159.

The Editor recommends...

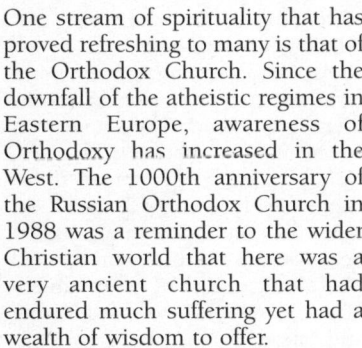

Naomi Starkey

From time to time we may sense that our personal way of prayer is proving less fruitful than formerly, or a friend or mentor may suggest that we could benefit from the insights of believers in a different faith context from our own. This is a valuable reminder (if we need one) that God is far bigger than our personal tastes and assumptions tend to make him.

One stream of spirituality that has proved refreshing to many is that of the Orthodox Church. Since the downfall of the atheistic regimes in Eastern Europe, awareness of Orthodoxy has increased in the West. The 1000th anniversary of the Russian Orthodox Church in 1988 was a reminder to the wider Christian world that here was a very ancient church that had endured much suffering yet had a wealth of wisdom to offer.

BRF has recently brought out a new edition of a book that has become a popular classic since its first publication in 1996: *The Jesus Prayer* by Bishop Simon Barrington-Ward. This book explores a key aspect of Orthodox spirituality. While the Jesus Prayer is in essence a simple form of words, it has been described as a way of entering into the river of prayer that flows from the heart of God.

Praying the Jesus Prayer can be experienced as joining with Christ himself as he continually prays for his people and the world he loves, in the presence of the Father. It is joining, too, with the Spirit of God who prays within the heart of each Christian 'with sighs too deep for words', for the healing and redemption of all things.

In his book, Simon Barrington-Ward draws on years of experience of praying the Jesus Prayer and teaching others to use it. He not only describes how to use the Jesus Prayer itself, but also provides biblical and historical background for understanding its significance. It is also interesting to note that through writing the original edition of *The Jesus Prayer*, he came to know Brother Ramon SSF, which led to their collaboration on *Praying the Jesus Prayer Together* (BRF, 2001), the last book that Brother Ramon wrote.

To order these books, please turn to the order form on page 159.

An extract from
Quiet Spaces: Fire

In this issue of BRF's prayer and spirituality journal, we focus on different aspects of fire. This powerful symbol appears many times in the Bible, particularly as an image for God himself, from the guiding pillar of fire at the time of the exodus to the tongues of flame on the Day of Pentecost. The following extract is a meditation written by Ann Persson on the fire of God's presence.

The purging fire

Imagine you're sitting by the fireside and watching, fascinated, as the flames dance in the grate, the wood spits and crackles and the soot on the chimneybreast glows and dies, forming ever-changing patterns. Turn the lights off and you have an even more magical experience. The room is both lit and warmed by the fire, and shadows move across the walls and ceiling.

Fire is a potent image in the Bible and a symbol of God's presence, as Moses discovered in the desert. God spoke to him from a burning bush and later guided the Israelites by a pillar of fire (Exodus 3:2; 13:21).

In the letter to the Hebrews it is written, 'Worship God acceptably with reverence and awe, for our "God is a consuming fire"' (Hebrews 12:28–29, NIV). This can feel scary but it is also his way

of refining us and deepening our relationship with him.

An incident comes to my mind from when I took part in an art therapy weekend. The theme was water and, in between the sessions, we were encouraged to be creative with a variety of media. As I worked on my own project, I became aware of one woman who was totally absorbed in building a boat out of scraps of card, string and fabric. It was about two feet long, very elegant and eventually painted all over in black, so that it looked like a funeral boat such as you might see in India.

In due course, she shared with the group that her mother had died when she was only 20 and now, ten years later, her father had died just nine months before our weekend. She was still deeply grieving and not quite sure how to move on in her life. After completing her boat, she knew what she needed to do, and that was to burn it prayerfully, in effect to let go of her grief and turn to face the future.

I will never forget standing beside her with two others as, solemnly, she set fire to her beautiful craft. I talked with her the other day, 13 years after the event, and she still looks back to that time as a defining, healing, pivotal moment in her life.

God desires to purify us of anything that would impede our progress as his disciples, and sometimes he uses challenging life circumstances to bring to the surface the fears, addictions or prejudices that need to be released.

The inner fire

When God poured out his Holy Spirit on the disciples, family and friends of Jesus at Pentecost, he accompanied his action with an outward sign of 'tongues of fire that… came to rest on each of them' (see Acts 2:3). When we dedicate our lives to God, he comes to live in us by his Holy Spirit. He lights a fire, as it were, within us. The inward fire of spiritual passion, power and love is his gift. I cannot produce it by myself, but my responsibility is to guard the flame.

This came home to me at the end of a three-day retreat. It had been a very inspirational time in which God had given me fresh insights and a real sense of his presence, which led to renewed commitment on my part. I was afraid that when I left, the experience might evaporate in the hurly-burly of daily life. In my final prayer time there, I had a picture of a lit candle with a guard around it and I wrote down these words in my journal: 'My mature responsibility is to guard the flame that God has lit within my heart, which the buffeting winds of life could so easily blow out.'

Sometimes we say that we feel 'burnt out'. Not surprisingly, this is often the experience of those in ministry who have to use many words and share many experiences but in whom the fire of God's Spirit is burning low. When the flame of a candle has become very small, it is usually because wax has built up around the sides and needs scraping back to give the wick more oxygen to burn brightly. When we are experiencing 'burn out' and circumstances seem to have snuffed out our sense of God's fire within us, we need to pay attention to what is happening. We need to take steps to cut back where possible; to give ourselves some 'time out' with God and room to breathe and recover.

Ann Persson, a BRF Trustee, has enjoyed leading Quiet Days over a period of many years. To find out more about Ann's Quiet Days, please contact the BRF office.

Quiet Spaces *is published three times a year, in March, July and November. To subscribe, please see the form on page 158.*

Praying with hands

Lucy Moore

If you're short of ideas for ways of encouraging children to pray, look no further than the *Barnabas* website. Go to www.barnabasinchurches.co.uk and click on the 'Ideas' menu tab. Here is just one example of the resources available, designed to help chidren connect Christian faith with their everyday life experiences.

Here is a simple reflective prayer time based on hands from an original idea by Michael Ford.

You'll need the Bible verses on cards as below and a big picture of a hand (or individual smaller hand outlines).

Introduction

Use the following facts and thoughts about hands to encourage children to see their hands in a new light.

How amazing are these two instruments on the ends of your arms! Imagine an advert for them:

- Beautiful water-resistant covering, tailored to your size.

- Breathable fabric and automatic cooling system, adaptable to a wide temperature range.

- Intelligent design: there are grey cells in the fingertips, same as for the brain, to aid piano playing, for instance.

- Opposing-thumb action: thousands of uses at work, at play, or around the home. Functions can include 'picking stuff up', 'writing', 'cooking', and 'hanging on for dear life'.

- Underpinned by carbon-calcium honeycomb-section alloy, stronger (pound-for-pound) than steel.

- Self-cleaning, self-repairing system with renewable energy supply.

- High sensitivity and fine control come as standard.

- There is even a 'gossamer-touch' option for those caring, sharing or playful moments.

- Safety features include pain-response reflex technology for extremes of heat, cold or pressure: automatic withdrawing if pain margins are exceeded.

- Standard lifetime guarantee.

Readings

Choose some of the following scriptures on 'hands' and print them on cards for children to read out, leaving a short pause between each. This could be done with a background of quiet instrumental music playing. Ask the children to listen out for the different ways hands are used in scripture. Whose hands are mentioned? (All Bible quotations taken from Today's New International Version.)

Who may ascend the mountain of the Lord? … Those who have clean hands and a pure heart.

PSALM 24:3–4

This is what the Lord says; '… See, I have engraved you on the palms of my hands.'

ISAIAH 49:8, 16

Whatever your hand finds to do, do it with all your might.

ECCLESIASTES 9:10

I will praise you as long as I live, and in your name I will lift up my hands.

PSALM 63:4

Activity

Display an outline of a large hand and pray together as below with suggestions from the whole group or give each child a handout of a hand outline to write or draw on individually.

Use the finger mnemonic for prayer to devise prayers for each finger:

Thumb: closest to your body when your hands are by your sides. Pray for those closest to you —your friends and family.

Index finger: pray for those whom others might point at rudely, people who are left out or hurting.

Middle finger: the tallest finger—pray for people in charge of countries, companies or schools.

Fourth finger: the weakest— pray for people who are ill.

Little finger: the smallest— pray for yourself.

Often in church, the minister raises his or her hands as a sign of blessing. Invite the children to hold out their hands now to show they are blessing each other and finish with these words:

'God be in your hands and in mine and in all we do with them today and for evermore. Amen'

Lucy Moore is an author, actor and storyteller, using her gifts as a member of the Barnabas *Ministry team.*

Guidelines © BRF 2008

The Bible Reading Fellowship
First Floor, Elsfield Hall, 15–17 Elsfield Way, Oxford OX2 8FG
Tel: 01865 319700; Fax: 01865 319701
E-mail: enquiries@brf.org.uk
Website: www.brf.org.uk

ISBN 978 1 84101 472 2

Distributed in Australia by:
Willow Connection, PO Box 288, Brookvale, NSW 2100.
Tel: 02 9948 3957; Fax: 02 9948 8153;
E-mail: info@willowconnection.com.au
Available also from all good Christian bookshops in Australia.
For individual and group subscriptions in Australia:
Mrs Rosemary Morrall, PO Box W35, Wanniassa, ACT 2903.

Distributed in New Zealand by:
Scripture Union Wholesale, PO Box 760, Wellington
Tel: 04 385 0421; Fax: 04 384 3990; E-mail: suwholesale@clear.net.nz

Distributed in Canada by:
The Anglican Book Centre, 80 Hayden Street, Toronto, Ontario, M4Y 3G2
Tel: 001 416 924-1332; Fax: 001 416 924-2760;
E-mail: abc@anglicanbookcentre.com; Website: www.anglicanbookcentre.com

Publications distributed to more than 60 countries

Printed in Singapore by Craft Print International Ltd

BRF is a Christian charity committed to resourcing the spiritual journey of adults and children alike. For adults, BRF publishes Bible reading notes and books and offers an annual programme of quiet days and retreats. Under its children's imprint *Barnabas*, BRF publishes a wide range of books for those working with children under 11 in school, church and home. BRF's *Barnabas Ministry* team offers INSET sessions for primary teachers, training for children's leaders in church, quiet days, and a range of events to enable children themselves to engage with the Bible and its message.

We need your help if we are to make a real impact on the local church and community. In an increasingly secular world people need even more help with their Bible reading, their prayer and their discipleship. We can do something about this, but our resources are limited. With your help, if we all do a little, together we can make a huge difference.

How can you help?

- You could support BRF's ministry with a donation or standing order (using the response form overleaf).

- You could consider making a bequest to BRF in your will, and so give lasting support to our work. (We have a leaflet available with more information about this, which can be requested using the form overleaf.)

- And, most important of all, you could support BRF with your prayers.

Whatever you can do or give, we thank you for your support.

BRF – resourcing your spiritual journey

BRF MINISTRY APPEAL RESPONSE FORM

Name _____

Address _____

_____ Postcode _____

Telephone _____ Email _____

(tick as appropriate)

Gift Aid Declaration

☐ I am a UK taxpayer. I want BRF to treat as Gift Aid Donations all donations I make from 6 April 2000 until I notify you otherwise.

Signature _____ Date _____

☐ I would like to support BRF's ministry with a regular donation by standing order (please complete the Banker's Order below).

Standing Order – Banker's Order

To the Manager, Name of Bank/Building Society _____

Address _____

_____ Postcode _____

Sort Code _____ Account Name _____

Account No _____

Please pay Royal Bank of Scotland plc, Drummonds, 49 Charing Cross, London SW1A 2DX (Sort Code 16-00-38), for the account of BRF A/C No. 00774151

The sum of _____ pounds on ___ /___ /___ (insert date your standing order starts) and thereafter the same amount on the same day of each month until further notice.

Signature _____ Date _____

Single donation

☐ I enclose my cheque/credit card/Switch card details for a donation of £5 £10 £25 £50 £100 £250 (other) £ _____ to support BRF's ministry

Credit/Switch card no. ☐☐☐☐☐☐☐☐☐☐☐☐☐☐☐☐☐☐☐
Expires ☐☐☐☐ Security code ☐☐☐ Issue no. of Switch card ☐☐☐☐

Signature _____ Date _____

(Where appropriate, on receipt of your donation, we will send you a Gift Aid form)

☐ Please send me information about making a bequest to BRF in my will.

Please detach and send this completed form to: Richard Fisher, BRF, First Floor, Elsfield Hall, 15–17 Elsfield Way, Oxford OX2 8FG. BRF is a Registered Charity (No.233280)

GL0108

Please note our subscription rates 2008–2009. From the May 2008 issue, the new subscription rates will be:

Individual subscriptions covering 3 issues for under 5 copies, payable in advance (including postage and packing):

		UK	SURFACE	AIRMAIL
GUIDELINES each set of 3 p.a.		£13.35	£14.55	£16.65
GUIDELINES 3-year sub	i.e. 9 issues	£30.00	N/A	N/A

Group subscriptions covering 3 issues for 5 copies or more, sent to ONE address (post free):

GUIDELINES   £10.80   each set of 3 p.a.

Please note that the annual billing period for Group Subscriptions runs from 1 May to 30 April.

Copies of the notes may also be obtained from Christian bookshops:

GUIDELINES   £3.60 each copy

SUBSCRIPTIONS

❏ Please send me a Bible reading resources pack to encourage Bible reading in my church
❏ I would like to take out a subscription myself (complete your name and address details only once)
❏ I would like to give a gift subscription (please complete both name and address sections below)

Your name _____

Your address _____

_____Postcode _____

Gift subscription name _____

Gift subscription address_____

_____Postcode _____

Please send *Guidelines* beginning with the May / September 2008 / January 2009 issue: (delete as applicable)

(please tick box)	UK	SURFACE	AIR MAIL
GUIDELINES	❏ £13.35	❏ £14.55	❏ £16.65
GUIDELINES 3-year sub	❏ £30.00		

I would like to take out an annual subscription to *Quiet Spaces* beginning with the next available issue:

(please tick box)	UK	SURFACE	AIR MAIL
QUIET SPACES	❏ £16.95	❏ £18.45	❏ £20.85

Please complete the payment details below and send your coupon, with appropriate payment, to: **BRF, First Floor, Elsfield Hall, 15–17 Elsfield Way, Oxford OX2 8FG.**

Total enclosed £ _____ (cheques should be made payable to 'BRF')

Payment by cheque ❏ postal order ❏ Visa ❏ Mastercard ❏ Switch ❏

Card number: ❏❏❏❏ ❏❏❏❏ ❏❏❏❏ ❏❏❏❏

Expires: ❏❏❏❏ Security code ❏❏❏ Issue no (Switch): ❏❏❏❏

Signature (essential if paying by credit/Switch card) _____

BRF is a Registered Charity

BRF PUBLICATIONS ORDER FORM

Please ensure that you complete and send off both sides of this order form.

Please send me the following book(s):

		Quantity	Price	Total
485 2	Journey to Jerusalem (*D. Winter*)	_____	£7.99	_____
574 3	Embracing God's World (*J. Huggett*)	_____	£7.99	_____
581 1	The Path of Celtic Prayer (*C. Miller*)	_____	£6.99	_____
509 6	The Jesus Prayer (*S. Barrington-Ward*)	_____	£4.99	_____
147 9	Praying the Jesus Prayer Together (*S. Barrington-Ward / Ramon*)	_____	£6.99	_____
538 5	My First Easter Sticker Book (*S.A. Wright*)	_____	£3.50	_____
455 5	The Story of Easter (*C. Doyle & J. Haysom*)	_____	£6.99	_____
560 6	Easter Days (*L. Lane*)	_____	£4.99	_____
031 1	PBC: Psalms 1—72 (*D. Coggan*)	_____	£8.99	_____
065 6	PBC: Psalms 73—150 (*D. Coggan*)	_____	£7.99	_____
027 8	PBC: Luke (*H. Wansbrough*)	_____	£7.99	_____
242 1	PBC: Ruth, Esther, Ecclesiastes, Song, Lamentations (*R. Fyall*)	_____	£8.99	_____
094 6	PBC: Job (*K. Dell*)	_____	£7.99	_____
092 2	PBC: James to Jude (*F.J. Moloney*)	_____	£7.99	_____
415 9	Quiet Spaces: Creation and Creativity (*Ed. B. Winter*)	_____	£3.99*	_____
448 7	Quiet Spaces: The Journey (*Ed. B. Winter*)	_____	£4.99	_____
449 4	Quiet Spaces: The Feast (*Ed. B. Winter*)	_____	£4.99	_____
450 0	Quiet Spaces: The Garden (*Ed. N. Starkey*)	_____	£4.99	_____
482 1	Quiet Spaces: The Wilderness (*Ed. N. Starkey*)	_____	£4.99	_____
483 8	Quiet Spaces: The City (*Ed. N. Starkey*)	_____	£4.99	_____
498 2	Quiet Spaces: Rock (*Ed. N. Starkey*)	_____	£4.99	_____
499 9	Quiet Spaces: Water (*Ed. N. Starkey*)	_____	£4.99	_____
500 2	Quiet Spaces: Fire (*Ed. N. Starkey*)	_____	£4.99	_____

Total cost of books £ _____

Donation £ _____

Postage and packing £ _____

TOTAL £ _____

POSTAGE AND PACKING CHARGES

order value	UK	Europe	Surface	Air Mail
£7.00 & under	£1.25	£3.00	£3.50	£5.50
£7.01–£30.00	£2.25	£5.50	£6.50	£10.00
Over £30.00	free	prices on request		

* Introductory offer

See over for payment details. All prices are correct at time of going to press, are subject to the prevailing rate of VAT and may be subject to change without prior warning.

PAYMENT DETAILS

Please complete the payment details below and send with appropriate payment and completed order form to:

**BRF, First Floor, Elsfield Hall,
15–17 Elsfield Way, Oxford OX2 8FG**

Name _____

Address _____

_____

_____ Postcode _____

Telephone _____

Email _____

Total enclosed £ _____(cheques should be made payable to 'BRF')

Payment by cheque ❏ postal order ❏ Visa ❏ Mastercard ❏ Switch ❏

Card number: ▢▢▢▢▢▢▢▢▢▢▢▢▢▢▢▢▢▢▢▢

Expires: ▢▢▢▢ Security code ▢▢▢ Issue no (Switch): ▢▢▢▢

Signature (essential if paying by credit/Switch card)_____

❏ Please do not send me further information about BRF publications.

ALTERNATIVE WAYS TO ORDER

Christian bookshops: All good Christian bookshops stock BRF publications. For your nearest stockist, please contact BRF.

Telephone: The BRF office is open between 09.15 and 17.30.
To place your order, phone 01865 319700; fax 01865 319701.

Web: Visit www.brf.org.uk

GL0108